Managing the sales organization

for the digitial age – International Edition

ANDERS SAHLGREN

ERIK SKOG

S✱S
sahlgrenskog.com

S&S Publishing
P.O. Box 3051
SE-103 61 Stockholm

Cover: Mark Belan
Graphic production: Whip Media
Printed by IngramSpark

ISBN 978-91-985116-2-8

CONTENT

3. The sales organization's productivity and its effect on the income statement 41

Part 2 - Model for managing sales organizations

4. DIMENSION 1: Territory management 51

5. DIMENSION 2: Target setting, follow-up & reward 65

6. DIMENSION 3: Visualizing the performance 83

PREFACE

Successful and attractive companies are profitable companies. Profitability is both a function of the external environment, where industry structure plays a central role, and the internal setting formed by the organization and leadership of the firm.

Good management, based on tactical decisions and a clear business model, is vital in implementing strategies and creating results. During my years as a strategy researcher, and through contacts with corporations and organizations in a wide variety of industries, I have seen good strategies combined with strong leadership and processes, but I have also seen the opposite, where planned strategies failed to be executed followed by poor results.

In any given industry you will always find a few firms doing a better job than others – often over extended time periods – and you ask yourself why. When one farmer drives new clean cars, the neighbor drives dirty old wrecks. They are both in the same industry following similar strategies, but success is about how well the strategies have been implemented. You can sum it up by saying that management tasks are 5% about analysis and choosing a strategy, and 95% about implementation.

The book you are now holding in your hand – "*Managing the Sales Organization for the digital age*" – will help you to lead and manage business-to-business sales organizations. It is aimed at university students in Business Administration, but is also a very practical management book for those involved in sales organizations and marketing.

I have taught strategy at the Stockholm School of Economics for 35 years, and it has struck me many times how little of the subject sales and its organization that is covered in the curriculum – in my own school as well as in other universities. This comprehensive and important book fills this gap.

The interaction between theory and practice is a key element in Business Administration. This book offers such a bridge, so please enjoy the book and benefit from the vast experiences presented by the authors in their "recipes".

Dr Örjan Sölvell
Professor of International Business at the Stockholm School of Economics
Senior Associate at the Institute for Strategy and Competitiveness at Harvard
Business School

About the book

How to increase performance and sales is a key question in most sales organizations. The perspective of this book is what the implications are for those managing the sales organizations in the digital age. Today, there are many new ways in approaching and servicing customers, complementing the personal approach of a sales force. The speed of change is high, information is readily available, and performance can be measured instantaneously. Taking this into consideration, the book describes which areas to address and what tools are available for management to improve performance in their sales organizations. The models described in the book are proven and based on academic research. Additionally, the models are further qualified through our decades of personal experiences as leaders for successful sales organizations and as management consultants. Under each area in the book, you will find practical examples of how companies have solved the various challenges in real life, as well as explanations of why it works with reference to marketing models, organizational theory and psychology.

The premise of the book is sales organizations with a sales force, wholly or partially, working in the field with business-to-business sales (B2B).

However, the book and its models are in many aspects applicable to other types of sales organizations, such as telemarketing organizations and sales forces aimed at consumers (B2C).

The parts of the book

The book is divided into three parts:

Part I provides basic knowledge of the sales organization. We describe its role, go through several common concepts and show the link between the sales organization's productivity and the company's income statement. Part I is primarily intended for readers who have no prior knowledge of marketing and sales organizations.

In part II we go through our model of how to analyze and influence the sales organization's productivity. The model describes nine performance areas, called dimensions, and the tools available for management to improve performance in each area. The nine dimensions are:

1. Territory management
2. Targets, follow-up and rewards
3. Visualizing the performance
4. Forecasting
5. Opportunity follow-up
6. Individual coaching and follow up
7. Activity levels and planning
8. Joint field visits
9. Performance improvement program

The model is based on practical experience in how to manage sales organizations and has been used as an analytical tool in several projects. We have conducted over a thousand interviews of sales people and sales managers at 150 companies in 15 countries where the model has been tested and well received. Under each dimension, we will give numerous examples to illustrate the problem areas and how different companies have handled the issues.

Part III provides ideas and methods on how to implement changes in the sales organization with the help of the model, as well as a number of other practical implementation tips.

Throughout the book, cases will be presented with anonymous companies from a wide variety of industries. These are primarily based on our own experiences.

Definitions

We would like to define some of the most frequent terms that appear throughout the book:

- **Customers** – both existing customers and potential customers, unless explicitly specified.

- **Sales people** – the people who are responsible for generating sales.

- **Sales force** – sales people out in the field, visiting customers.

- **Sales manager** – the person to whom the sales people report. Both sales person and sales manager may in some organizations have other titles.

- **Sales district** – all the customers that the sales person is responsible for. Districts do not necessarily need to be structured geographically, they can also be, for example, by customer industry segment.

PART 1

The Sales organization

CHAPTER 1

The role of the sales organization

The sales organization is the part of the company that actively sells the company's products, i.e. its goods and services. An example of how a sales organization can be organized is described in figure 1.1, below. In addition to the sales people in the field visiting customers, a sales organization could also consist of other roles. Sales support will assist the sales people with in-depth technical knowledge. Telesales will complement the field sales and work the customer base by phone. Administration will support the organization in using the IT-systems, reporting system, etc.

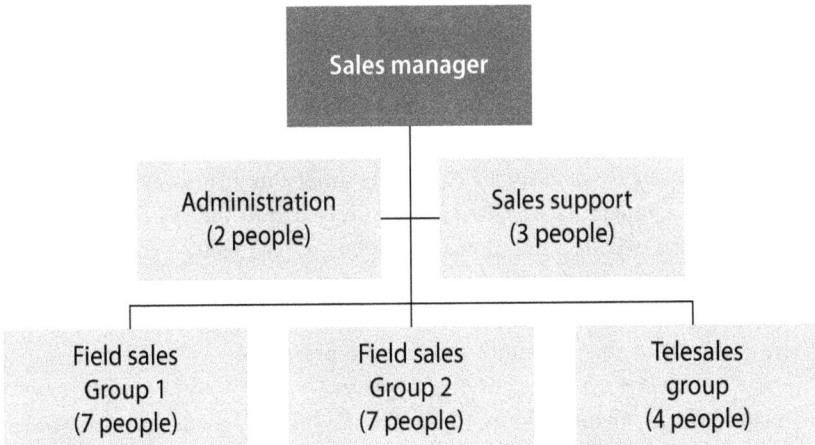

Figure 1.1 Example of a sales organization, consisting of two sales groups operating in the field and one telesales group. Two functions are supporting the sales groups: Sales support provides technical sales competence and administration gives support in using IT-systems and reporting.

In this chapter, we will cover the following aspects of the sales organization:

- What is personal selling
- Pros and cons with a sales force
- The company's channel strategy
- The role of sales management

What is personal selling?

Personal selling is when a sales person, in personal contact with a customer, makes that customer see the situation in the way the sales person wants. This is a broad definition and the same psychology can be used in other circumstances when a person wishes to influence another person.

The sales profession has evolved with the development and understanding of psychology. The area has also, when it comes to more complex sales, developed together with analysis and understanding of customers' purchasing processes and needs.

Historical development

Three distinct breakthroughs can be distinguished in the development, which has led us to the professional sales role and the professional sales organization of today.[1]

The first breakthrough was an early form of personal selling with traveling representatives in the USA, signing orders on insurance policies or capital equipment. Part of the task was to return to the customers on a weekly basis to collect premiums or instalment payments.

When they were successful enough, all their time was spent on collecting payments and there was no time left to sign up new customers. Then it was decided that the more successful representatives should concentrate on signing up more customers – sales – and have other colleagues collect the payments. The professional sales force, which only worked with selling, was born.

The second breakthrough came with the publication of "The Psychology of Selling" 1925, written by E.K. Strong. Strong introduced concepts like features and benefits, objection handling, open questions and closing

---

techniques. These concepts are still in use and are generally called "sales techniques".

During the 1970s came the next breakthrough with proven and standardized sales methodologies in more complex sales situations. "SPIN Selling" is regarded as the first example, but many more followed, such as "Consultative selling", "Strategic selling", "Solution Selling" and more.

Whether we now stand before a fourth breakthrough is debatable and remains to be seen. "The Challenger Sale", where sales people challenge the customers' views and provide them with new insights, is a theory that claims this. The concept is based on research from successful sales behaviors.

The area "personal selling" focuses on developing the skills and knowledge of the sales person. Examples of these are sales technique, negotiation and closing skills, knowledge about the market, the customers and the products. Methodology for how to approach the customers and how to develop business opportunities and the customer relations are also quite often covered.

Successful companies with field sales organizations usually have training programs and common concepts and language to develop and maintain a high level of competence among their sales people. The area is well documented and there are many training programs in this field.

This book is focusing on the *management* of the sales organization and we will not further discuss personal selling skills other than in the management and organizational context.

Pros and cons with a sales force

To work with a sales force, where the sales people visit and have a direct contact with customers, has many benefits:

- The company gets a direct, personal two-way communication with the customer.
- It is possible to convey a complex message in an interactive way.
- How to sell can be adapted to each individual customer.
- The company gets a clear and personal contact, facing the customer.

It's a powerful way to the market: You visit, identify needs, convince and close the business with the customer.

The drawback is that it's an expensive way to reach the market. Salaries and expenses for a sales organization are usually high, and management and support functions need to be in place in order to take advantage of its strengths.

How you structure and manage the sales organization, i.e. how you utilize this valuable resource, is the topic of this book. To put it differently: How do you maximise the return on the investment you put in a sales organization?

The company's channel strategy

The sales force is one of many channel options in establishing contact with the customers and generating sales. It's an important part of the company strategy to evaluate and select the right channels suitable for their specific situation. Another part of this process is deciding and allocating the necessary resources in operating these channels. This is what frequently is called the company's channel strategy.

The different channel options are illustrated in figure 1.2, below.

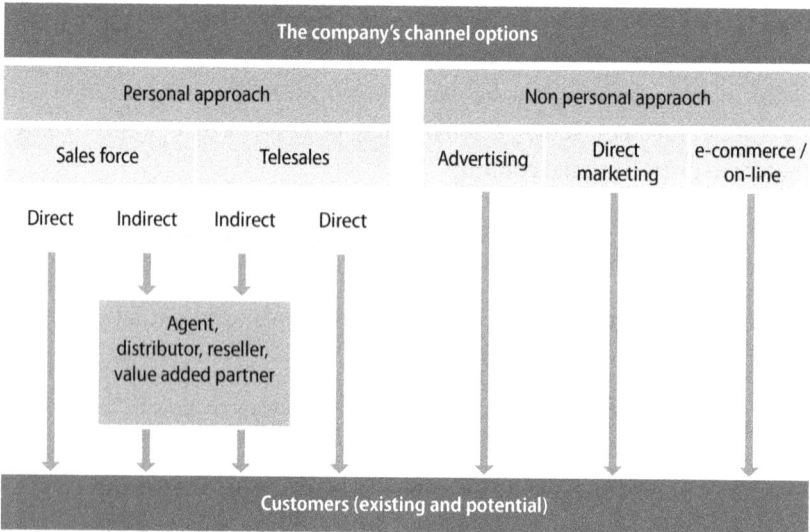

Figure 1.2 The company could choose one or several channels when approaching the customers. (Adapted from Zoltners & Sinha, 2001[2])

As the figure shows you can have a personal or non-personal approach to the customers. The personal approach could be done through a sales force or through telesales, and both these channels come in two versions: *Direct sales*, when you approach and sell to the end customer with your own sales people, and *indirect sales*, where your sales people sell through a third party, who in their turn sell to the end customer. Examples of these third parties are resellers, such as agents (independent representatives for the company in a certain market), distributors (keeping inventory and supplying the company's products to their customers) and value-added partners (adding value to the company's products before selling it to their customers).

The personal approach could be substituted or complemented by a non-personal approach. Here, channel examples are advertising (creates an interest for the company's products), direct marketing (sending material directly to the customers to encourage them to contact the company and order the products, e.g. catalogue sales) and e-commerce. These channels are sometimes under the management and control of the sales organization, sometimes they are separate and report to other functions in the company.

It's common for companies to have a *multichannel* strategy, where they choose to approach the market in different ways.

Channel selection

There are a couple of factors dictating the most suitable channel option:

- **Complexity of the offering.** More complex products and services require a close, personal interaction with the customer in order to understand the needs and designing the right solution.
- **Geographical presence.** Do you need to be present in a geographical market yourself, or could you solve this with an indirect channel partner representing your company? Or could you approach the customers in this geography using another channel, such as telesales or e-commerce?

The on-line company that introduced a sales force

The founders of the IT company were early in realizing that IT hardware such as PCs, printers and accessories could be sold through mail order and their catalogue had a wide distribution in the corporate market. When e-commerce had a breakthrough in the 1990s the success continued on-line. They were now a strong supplier on the Swedish market and they expanded to the other Nordic countries. The fact that they kept their strong position intact, despite competitors from bigger European countries such as UK and Germany, impressed the industry analysts.

However, with the competitive pressure, the profitability started to deteriorate on the standard products and the company saw an opportunity to recapture profitability by selling larger solutions comprising of servers, networks and installation services. They did not have a good track record on these more complex products, which in most of the cases were sold by competitors that had a direct, personal contact with the with customers. To succeed, they needed to be in direct contact with the customers to fully understand their needs and to be able to discuss and design the right solutions. This, they could not achieve with their web shop

There were many long discussions in the management team on this topic. Their success model had been based on making products easily available at competitive prices, without needing a big direct sales organization working the customers. Those were the type of companies they had been taking market share from throughout the years.

The market size for the more complex solutions and the profitability potential were analyzed. They decided that, despite their history, the time was right to establish a direct sales force for the customer segments that required bigger and more complex solutions. Once this was in place, and after recruitments and training programs, sales started to pick up at a good pace and their profitability improved.

- **The size of the customer.** Customer size can influence the channel selection. Small customers are to a larger extent handled through telesales, whereas large customers are more frequently dealt with by direct field sales organizations. Since a direct field sale is costly, there must be a good profitability potential of the customer to justify this channel. This requires the customer to be of a certain size.

- **Phases in the sales process.** Certain phases in the sales process may call for the sales person to be present, but you may question whether it is necessary for the sales person to be present in *all* phases. In an introductory phase the customers themselves may collect information and generate interest for the company's solution, while it may require a contact with the sales person to execute the deal. Thereafter the customers may have the knowledge and capacity themselves to handle additional orders.

The industrial company opened new channels

That the customer should have *one* point of contact was the philosophy of the company that sold welding equipment to the manufacturing and automotive industry. The company had a long history of bringing innovations to the market and was in the technical forefront of its industry. A knowledgeable and well-trained sales representative handled all the contacts with the customer. Nursing the relationship was a key ingredient in retaining the customers and keeping the competitors out. As a result, the same person had throughout the years also serviced the customer's small additional orders. They filled in the order form and sent it to the order department, which was entered into the order system.

Over the years, the additional orders became an increasing source of irritation for both the customer and the sales person. For the customer, it was difficult to reach the sales person and place the order, since the sales person was travelling and in meetings. For the sales person, it was disruptive when torn away from the main duties of selling new production lines to administrate orders of low amounts.

By surveying the customers' perceptions and collecting input from the sales force, the management could change the service model, and adapt it to a more cost efficient and service friendly model.

The solution was to open a self-service channel for the customers, where they through a web login or through a customer service desk, could place their orders without having to involve the sales person.

Figure 1.3 illustrates how the two last factors – customer size and sales phase – interact when choosing sales channel[3]. Below the dotted line, a direct sales force is used; above the line other channels are used to interact with the customer.

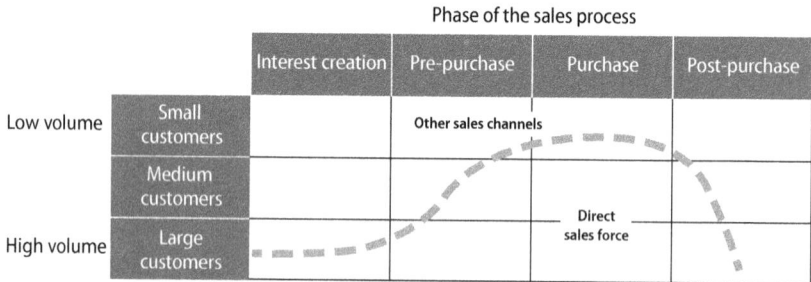

Phase of the sales process

		Interest creation	Pre-purchase	Purchase	Post-purchase
Low volume	Small customers		Other sales channels		
	Medium customers				
High volume	Large customers			Direct sales force	

Figure 1.3 The most appropriate channel option depends on what stage in the sales process, and how big the customer is. A direct sales force is used under the dotted line, where the costs for this approach can be justified. Other, more cost efficient channels, are used above the dotted line. (Adapted from Zoltner & Sinha, 2001).

The role of Sales management

Overall responsibility

The sales management's overall responsibility is to make the sales organization work with the right customers, with the highest possible activity level, and with the best possible quality. This summary is applicable to the sales management role irrespective of the size of the organization or the organization level the manager operates from. In larger sales organizations there could be several management levels such as team leaders, regional sales managers, and sales directors.

Good management is critical in all types of organizations, but there are certain characteristics worth noting when managing sales organizations.

- **The results of the individuals are often easy to measure**. How well a sales person performs is often visible to the rest of the organization, which to a greater extent makes the person exposed to viewpoints and assessments from others (even outside their own department).

- **A sales person gets more "no" than "yes" in their work.** A sales person working with many different business opportunities is likely to win only a small portion of these. This can be mentally trying and requires support and coaching.

- **A sales person has a wide exposure both externally to customers and internally in their own organization.** Enthusiasm, or on the other side, dissatisfaction, could easily spread both internally and externally.

- **Sales people are typically well paid compared to other roles in the company.** To maximize the return on this investment is therefore especially important.

Other responsibilities when managing sales organizations

This book focuses on the management of sales people. There are, however, other responsibilities that may be part of the sales management's role, for example:

- **Hiring and termination of sales people.** To recruit sales people with the right qualifications is part of the management's responsibilities, as well as handling the situation when you are forced to terminate or outplace a sales person.

- **Training of sales people.** Making sure that the sales person has the right competence to sell the products and services of the company is another area. This concerns both product training and trainings in sales technique or sales methodology. Sometimes it's the manager who is the trainer, but more frequently other internal or external resources do this.

- **Develop the company's business proposition.** The experience and feedback the sales people have from their customers are naturally channelled through the sales manager. If the company finds it difficult to get acceptance for what they offer, there could be a need to revise and adapt their message to the customers, or even change the business proposition altogether. In this case the sales manager would normally play a key role.

- **Lead generation**. The lead generation can be delegated to many of the roles within a sales organization. This task may sometimes fall to the sales people, while other times it falls to the marketing function or the sales manager. All of these roles, however, will often be involved in the task.

- **The manager having customers of his own**. Besides the role of managing the sales people's approach to the market, the manager may be responsible for his own customers, having a sales district himself.

Summary

The sales organization is the part of the company actively selling its products and services. It consists of sales people, support functions and management positions. Personal selling is a high-quality channel to the market, but it's expensive. The benefits with a personal selling approach – the ability to convey complex messages, to adapt both the message and the solution to the customer specific needs and to present a personal face to the customer – should be weighed against alternative channels to the market. The channel strategy is influenced by the customer size, the complexity of the offering, and the stages of the sales process. Many companies use more than one channel to the market, where they complement each other.

The sales management's overall responsibility is to make the sales organization work with the right customers with the highest possible activity level and with the best possible quality in order to maximize the return of the sales force investment.

CHAPTER 2

Basic concepts when managing sales people

In this chapter we will cover some basic concepts you are likely to encounter when discussing sales organizations. These are:

- Sales process
- Sales pipeline and sales funnel
- CRM system
- The quality and quantity concepts in sales

Sales process

The sales process depicts how a company conducts its business, describing the activities the sales people need to do to generate sales. The company's sales process reflects the customer's buying process, which are the steps the buyer takes before making a purchase decision.

What the sales process looks like varies depending on *what* you sell and to *whom* you sell.

- **What you sell:** Complex products, and products that are purchased infrequently, have longer cycles and consist of more steps. As an example, it takes longer time to sell an IT-system than office supplies.
- **To whom you sell:** Customers with regulated purchase behaviors or more decision makers lead to longer cycle times and longer processes.

As an example, it takes longer time to sell to a large public sector organization, where legal requirements regulate the process, than selling to a small company, where the decision maker and the user could be the same person.

This also holds true for buying behaviors on the consumer market. It's a considerably more complex process buying a house than a carton of milk. When buying a house, you look at a house, you report interest, you may look at it a second time, you check your financing capability, you submit a bid, you do an inspection, you negotiate the final price, you sign the contract and finally, you pay. When buying a carton of milk, you simply buy a carton of milk.

Generic sales processes in B2B

Below you will find a couple of examples illustrating how companies conduct their business. A company can work with more than one process when approaching their market. For example, a company selling printing solutions may have one sales process for the system (comprising of hardware, software and services), another sales process for selling toner and consumables, and it may all be regulated by a frame agreement.

Deal driven sales process

In this process sales are generated through deals, which the sales people drive from the first contact with the customer until the final order. The revenue comes from the order the sales person signs with the customer. It is a one-time order, but sometimes additional orders, associated with the deal, are placed at a later stage.

An example where this process is used is when selling IT-systems. The sales person (who sells this system all the time) is usually the one guiding the buyer (who rarely or never has bought this system) through the process. It is common that several people from the customer will be involved in the decision-making process, as the system may influence different roles on the customer side.

A process could look like this:

1. **Qualification of the customer.** Is there a budget allocated for the project and/or is there interest from the customer, making it worthwhile to pursue the opportunity?
2. **Need.** What are the needs of the involved parties at the customer side, such as the users, the IT department and the financial decision maker?
3. **Specification.** What does the sales person offer the customer?
4. **Demonstration and references.** How does the solution work practically? Either in a demonstration environment or at another, similar customer.
5. **Proposal.** What price, delivery time, and other terms apply for buying the system?
6. **Signed agreement.** Customer and supplier agree on terms and conditions, and the deal will be invoiced.

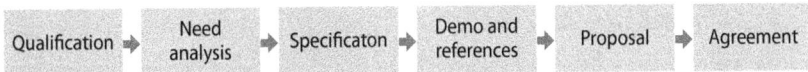

Figure 2.1 Example from a deal driven process, where the sales person drives the deal from the first contact to the order. Several activities have to take place before the customer can sign the agreement.

Procurement driven sales process

Supplier and customer first agree on terms before the supplier will start delivering. The sale (and revenue) is preceded by a contract where the parties agree on the price, volume and other terms first. When the contract is completed and signed, the customer can start ordering the products and services according to the contract.

The sales person is involved in the process leading up to the signing of the agreement, but is generally not involved in the orders that follow, which are usually handled by other functions of the supplier (customer service, order department, web shop, electronic data interchange - EDI, etc.). Orders and revenue will come repeatedly, on many different occasions, throughout the contract time. This type of process can be found where the supplier satisfies an on-going, regular need of the customer.

Overall the process steps are similar whether you sell direct or indirect material. However, it differs in the time and effort spent in each stage. There is a difference when an automotive customer procures chairs to use in their cars (direct materials), compared to office chairs that are used for internal, office purposes (indirect materials). Direct material is often more demanding in needs analysis and specification. The customer in this case is generally the party setting the pace and controlling the process.

The process could look like this:

1. Need analysis

2. Specification of desired product or service

3. Test/certification – more common when purchasing direct material

4. Agreement – Volumes, prices, length of agreement, etc. are agreed between the parties.

5. Subsequent orders

6. Follow-up – The follow-up allows the customer to bring up delivery quality and the sales person to verify that the customer is procuring the agreed volume. Follow-ups like this are very common when selling direct material, but following up the customers purchase commitments is also advisable when selling indirect material.

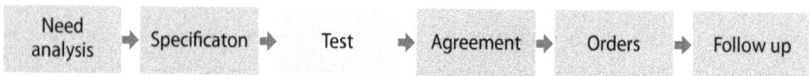

Need analysis ➡ Specificaton ➡ Test ➡ Agreement ➡ Orders ➡ Follow up

Figure 2.2 Example from a procurement driven sales process. First the parties agree on price, volume and other terms. When the agreement is signed the customer is able to start ordering the products for the duration of the contract.

Frame agreement

Frame agreements are done by large customers or by coalitions of customers with similar needs. The purpose of the frame agreement is to negotiate favorable terms for the purchasing customers and to simplify future purchases for both customers and suppliers, since terms and conditions (including prices) already are agreed upon. For the supplier, the frame agreement is no guarantee for any sales; it only provides an opportunity to approach the customers affiliated to the agreement. It can be regarded as a hunting license; sales people from the contracted companies get a license to hunt for business for the duration of the agreement. Since there is usually more than one supplier in frame agreements, there is still competition. There is certainly less competition than on the open market, but all of them are qualified. The revenues will come only after a customer, under the agreement, has purchased and placed the order at the supplier.

The process is in two steps – in the first step you are accepted as a supplier, in the second step you do your business.

STEP 1: Approved supplier

- **Need analysis.** The overall needs among the participating customers under the agreement are reviewed.

- **Specification.** Description of the products and services they intend to purchase during the term of the contract.

- **Request for proposal.** Being sent out to many potential suppliers, based on the specifications.

- **Proposal.** Sent in by the potential suppliers.

- **Agreement.** Suppliers are selected and signed. Terms and conditions are stipulated in the agreement.

STEP 2: Sales

- **Purchase decision** of a participating customer under the agreement

---

- **Specific need** for this customer
- **Specified solution**
- **Simplified proposal** (price and terms according to frame agreement)
- **Accept** (no separate agreement necessary). After this delivery and invoicing.

Step 1. Approved supplier

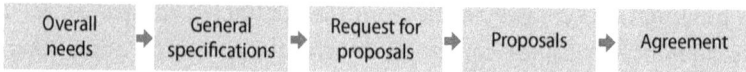

| Overall needs | → | General specifications | → | Request for proposals | → | Proposals | → | Agreement |

Step 2. Sales

| Purchase decision | → | Specific needs | → | Specified solution | → | Simplified proposal | → | Accept |

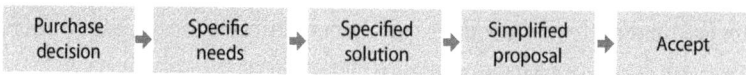

Figure 2.3 Example of a frame agreement process in two steps. Firstly, the companies have to be approved as suppliers before they, in the second step, can start selling their products and services to the customers.

No process

There are also industries where there is no need for a step-by-step sales process. Orders (or no orders) are taken every time the sales person and the buyer meet.

This is common when selling fast moving consumables to retail outlets, such as grocery chains, and small service companies, such as hairdressers. During the visit or contact with the customer, the sales person will do all the activities necessary to generate the sale: presenting the offer, checking inventory status, negotiate, and placing the order.

The sales person will return periodically to the customer to do business again, checking that the customer has enough products and to inform about new products and campaigns. (Note that there may be a frame agreement regulating terms and conditions even here – especially when you sell to the major grocery chains).

Sales pipeline and sales funnel

Future business opportunities are often described as a sales pipeline or a sales funnel. A sales pipeline, as the one in figure 2.4, illustrates how the opportunities are in different stages of maturity before they will produce an order (this is related to the sales process concept we covered earlier in this chapter).

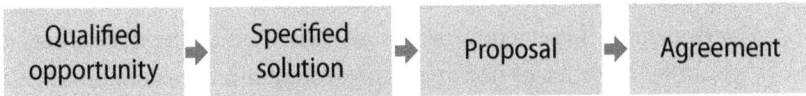

| Qualified opportunity | ➡ | Specified solution | ➡ | Proposal | ➡ | Agreement |

Figure 2.4 A sales pipeline describing different stages of a business opportunity.

Since a lot of the opportunities a company works with will fall away in different stages of maturity, it is fairer to talk about a sales funnel. How big a portion of the opportunities you succeed in progressing, or converting, to the next stage is called conversion rate. Conversion rate (in percentage) could either be measured between two different stages, as figure 2.5 shows below, or between the first stage and the last stage, where the conversion rate will be a factor of the conversion of all individual stages.

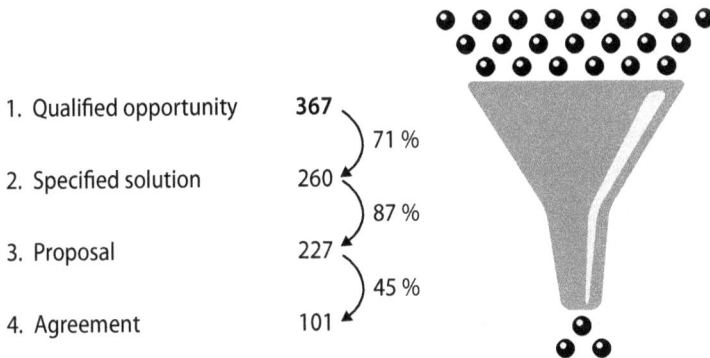

1. Qualified opportunity	367	
		71 %
2. Specified solution	260	
		87 %
3. Proposal	227	
		45 %
4. Agreement	101	

Figure 2.5 Sales funnel showing the number of opportunities in different stages. Between the stages conversion rates are shown, indicating the percentage of opportunities progressing to the next stage.

Since the funnel reveals where in the process you lose opportunities, it's a good tool for analyzing how well the sales people are in developing the business, and what actions need to be applied to increase sales:

- **Higher conversion of opportunities.** If sales people have a low conversion rate between different stages in the funnel, it's reasonable to question what could be done to improve the success rate. If you have a low conversion rate between proposal and agreement, you may want to review how proposals are being presented. If a single sales person has a lower conversion rate compared to the colleagues, it could be a matter of improving presentation and negotiation skills for that sales person. If it's a common problem for the entire sales force, the attractiveness of what is being offered could be questioned. (If you, as in figure 2.5, win almost half of the proposals, it is not a bad situation if there are many suppliers submitting proposals).

- **Fill up with even more opportunities.** To keep the sales at a constant level, you always need to fill the funnel with new opportunities at a certain rate. If you want to increase sales you need to *further* increase this inflow of new opportunities. Given constant conversion rates, you can *always* increase sales by further increasing the inflow of new opportunities.

CRM systems

CRM systems (Customer Relationship Management), sometimes referred to as sales force automation systems, are IT based tools helping sales organizations to keep track of customers and business opportunities as well as facilitating sales planning and reporting. In this chapter, we will cover the following:

- What sales organizations hope to achieve with these systems
- What are the parts comprising the systems
- Important aspects when implementing the systems

What sales organizations hope to achieve

These IT-based systems will automate the work of the sales people, and the increased productivity will of course benefit the whole company. But the sales people's personal productivity is only part of the equation. For the management of the sales organization it is also about securing a structure and providing support in managing and controlling the business.

Structure

A fundamental need when managing a sales organization is to secure the information about the customers and to avoid being too dependent on each individual sales person. What will happen if you let sales people handle critical customer information in their own personal way? What happens if some sales people neglect this task, or if some even quit the company? Do you then risk losing the customer? For these reasons, it's important to satisfy the following needs:

- **The customer structure.** An overview of all the customers you, as a company, are approaching, marked with which sales person is responsible for which customers. This will allow you to group customers and to reallocate customers between sales people.
- **Information about every customer.** Basic information per customer such as name, address, points of contact, important information taken from meetings and other contact with a customer, as well as the currently pursued business opportunities with the customer. Also of interest is the purchase history, which most likely is retrieved from other systems (ERP system, invoicing system).
- **Access to critical documents.** Contracts, proposals, and other agreements with the customer should be easily accessible.

Management support and control

The CRM systems provide a greater transparency of the day-to-day work of the sales people, making it easier for management to follow-up:

- **Follow-up of business opportunities.** Showing a picture of the all business opportunities the sales people drive, but also a detailed view of each opportunity; which customer, how much value and which stage of maturity.

- **Follow-up of activities.** Allowing access to activity information; i.e. how many customer visits did the sales people do, with whom did they meet and what was the result of the visits.

- **Reporting.** Provides a tool for sales people and managers, simplifying when producing reports.

Comprising parts

Parts of the CRM systems are the tools sales people also use in a manual system before implementing an IT based system. These are:

- Customer card, with contact information
- Calendar
- List of business opportunities
- Document archive

Furthermore, the systems also contain functions improving the personal productivity for the sales person, and tools for management control and reporting:

- Connecting information on customers and business opportunities to e-mail systems, electronic calendars and other functions such as reminders and to-do-lists.
- Logging of important events
- Sales funnel (business opportunities in certain stages of maturity)

Important aspects when implementing

Before implementation

Implementing a CRM system does not automatically mean that sales people start working professionally. If they have worked in an environment without transparency and without reporting, there is nothing to suggest that they would work differently, just because a system was implemented

It is highly recommendable to first establish reporting, follow-up procedures, and good information quality of customers in the manual world, *before* implementing the IT based system.

The CRM system in itself does not create a professional sales organization, but it can offer great support in automating the work for those organizations already working professionally.

The company that re-launched its CRM system

The company, which sold environmental equipment to the manufacturing industry (extractors, fans, etc.) had new owners that wanted to see a greater professionalism in the sales operations. The CEO, who also was the founder of the company, was skilled in both acquiring new customers and developing the existing ones. He had led the sales group of eight sales people in an informal way for several years. He now appointed the best sales person as sales manager.

The newly appointed manager had been at the company since he left high school. He now listened to friends and did some research on the web how to make the sales group more productive. He concluded that if he implemented a CRM system, the information structure and the management processes should fall in place.

After nine months, it was clear that not much had changed. Some of the sales people used the system extensively and the CEO's feeling was that perhaps they spent more time administrating than meeting customers. Other sales people did not use the system at all, they complained on deficiencies and lack of user friendliness in the system and frequently asked, "Should we sell or administrate".

It was the CFO of the company that was able to formulate the problem: "It's as if I would start using an IT based accounting system when all the papers were in one big mess and when we didn't have an account plan. First you need to get the papers in order, decide the account plan and approval procedures, etc. – then you implement the IT system."

The company decided to make a restart focusing on the routines for the sales group. They paused the use of the CRM system, defined reporting routines and meeting formats and frequency, and worked in that way for six months before reintroducing the CRM system, now successfully.

When using the systems

When sales organizations aren't getting the desired results from the systems, we usually give the following advice:

- **Establish and follow-up the minimum requirements in using the system.** Taking full advantage of the CRM system requires *all* the sales people to *continuously* update the system. Otherwise, management will not get an accurate picture of the business opportunities that the sales organization is currently driving. The sales management must decide what information the sales people have to fill in, and how often this should be done, and they need to follow up that sales people adhere to these minimum levels. Management should also be clear on their specific needs. These do not always coincide with the sales people's need for personal productivity, but they should nevertheless be met.

- **Establish maximum levels in using the system.** On the other hand, there's a risk for some sales people to be engulfed by irrelevant parts of the systems or spend an excessive amount of time on administration (at the expense of productive sales activities). In these instances, there are good grounds for limiting the usage. Either through blocking some of the functionality (just because the functionality is there, doesn't mean you should use it), or by limiting how much can be written in different fields.

- **CRM systems do not replace reporting and follow-up.** A common mistake, after implementing the system, is to believe you no longer need to follow up on the sales people in person, and that it would suffice to produce a report from the system. If you take away the physical meeting with the sales person, you take away the opportunity for the sales person to explain his or her performance and for the management to understand and ensure the quality of the business opportunities and customer activities the sales person has reported into the system. The system will, however, automate the production of the report for the sales person before the follow-up meeting with the manager.

The terms quality and quantity in sales

Quality and quantity are terms that sales organizations often use to describe their work. Quite often will the terms be polarized where you will get the impression that the choice is either/or. But what do the terms stand for and how do they relate to each other?

Quantity means that the sales people have high activity levels, do a lot of customer calls, generate many business opportunities, and will close a high number of deals thanks to having a large number of opportunities. There is a strong focus on measuring and following up on activities.

Quality means that the sales people work with the right type of customers and the right type of business opportunities. The skillset of the sales people is in focus, and they rely on their ability to win a large proportion of the deals.

How the terms relate to each other

To polarize the issue, where you must choose between either quality or quantity is incorrect. They are *not* mutually exclusive. Productive sales organizations perform well in both aspects. The model in figure 2.6 illustrates how these two attributes co-exist in different type of organizations.

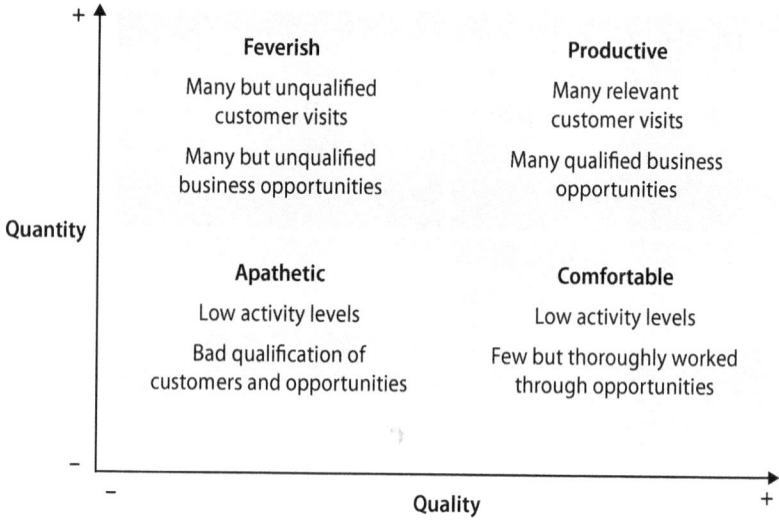

Figure 2.6 Co-existence of quality and quantity in sales.

Apathetic

Low activity combined with low quality in execution. In these organizations, the sales effort is reactive and only responding to incoming requests. These organizations will only survive where demand greatly exceeds supply or in monopolistic situations. When competition hardens, they will struggle to survive.

Feverish

These organizations have high activity levels when working the customer base, but without questioning the quality of the customer. The measure of success is a lot of customer calls. They may even visit customers too small to justify having a sales person calling on them. The business opportunities generated are not properly evaluated, and their closing percentage is low. But since they generate a lot of opportunities, they count on winning enough of them to keep going.

Comfortable

These organizations have a low tempo in working the customer base. They work with few customers and few business opportunities, on which they spend a lot of time. Their ability to break new ground and find new opportunities is limited. They make it a virtue to be quality focused which means they spend a lot of effort on the customers and opportunities they *do* have, rather than finding the ones they *should* have. The organization is in a comfort zone where they would rather spend the extra time on already well developed opportunities than on going out in un-known territory, finding new customers and opportunities.

Since the comfortable sales organizations create few business opportunities, the pressure is stronger to win these. If you are under strong pressure to win a case, perhaps at "any cost", it will lead to a poor negotiation climate with the customer. Even if you have developed the case in all possible ways, you may still end up making concessions in order to win it (i.e. by lowering prices).

Productive

Productive sales organizations have both quality and quantity in the way they work.

With quality, we mean that these organizations ensure that the sales people are working with the right type of customers, that there are good processes and methods to prioritize customers and business opportunities, and that they secure a high skillset among their sales people.

With quantity, we mean these organizations also ensure that the sales people work with the right intensity in order to make or exceed their goals: That they have enough opportunities, enough proposals, enough customers and that they make enough customer calls to make this happen. These are all measurable activities, and the productive sales organizations pay attention and follow up on these.

There is also a combination effect of quality and quantity worth noting. Since the productive sales organization continuously approach new customers, it can continuously evaluate and select the most attractive business opportunities to work on. Quantity, in this case, leads to quality.

Summary

The sales process is a description of how a company conducts its business. It reflects the customer's purchasing process, the steps the customer needs to take before being able to buy. How the process looks depends on what you sell and to whom you sell. One can discern a few different types of general sales processes in business-to-business sales: deal driven, procurement driven and frame agreement driven sales.

The sales process describes how far you have come in a business opportunity, and when you analyze a number of business opportunities you usually talk about a "pipeline" or "sales funnel". The "sales funnel" is a more suitable term than "pipeline" since it better illustrates how business opportunities gradually fall away. A defined sales process is a good foundation when managing sales organization.

Common tools in sales organizations are customer relationship management systems (CRM), sometimes also called sales force automation systems (SFA). These IT-based systems increase the personal productivity for the sales person as well as provides transparency, structure and control for the management of the sales force.

There are quality and quantity aspects in sales. Quantity means that you have a high activity level, making it possible to work with many customers and many business opportunities. Quality means that you work with the right type of customers, with the right type of opportunities and that the sales people have the right skillsets to win a high portion of the opportunities. A productive sales organization has both a high level of quality and a high level of quantity in the way they work.

© ANDERS SAHLGREN & ERIK SKOG

CHAPTER 3

The sales organization's productivity and its effect on the income statement

Increasing revenue is usually the most important issue for a sales organization, which is influenced by how productive the organization is. For those managing the sales organization, productivity is a matter of getting the maximum out of the cost they have invested in the sales force. In other words, making certain the sales people work with high quality and at a high pace (quantity).

How to increase productivity and thereby free capacity, and how that could translate to the income statement, is the subject of this chapter.

Current working capacity

When increasing productivity, it's first necessary to understand the current capacity of the sales organization, or put differently, what *effort* the sales organization makes to generate sales. For the case of simplicity, we measure this effort in the number of customer visits the organization makes. (A similar analysis could be applied on outbound phone calls for a tele-sales organization). These customer visits are made for two reasons:

- **Securing customer loyalty.** These are the recurring visits sales people do to maintain the customer relationships and to ensure customer loyalty in order to make the customer keep on buying in the future. How many visits they make depend on the number of customers they have, and with what frequency these are approached.

- **Generate and drive business.** The sales people make these visits to generate and drive business deals. How many deals the sales people are able to make during a year depend on the number of visits they need to do in order to win the deal, and how often they win in relation to the total number of deals they participate in. Knowing the estimated average revenue per deal, you can then calculate the total annual revenue for the organization.

What this analysis tells you is the capacity the sales organization has to approach a certain number of customers and the capacity to drive a certain number of deals, and what revenue this will generate.

Number of visits generated by the organization	
10 sales people making 160 visits per person and year	1,600 visits
Number of visits consumed by the organization	
I: To secure customer loyalty	
50 major customers visited 4 times/year	200 visits
200 other customers visited 2 times/year	400 visits
II: To drive business deals	
Participating in 300 deals where the customer is visited 2 times on average before losing the deal	600 visits
Participating in 100 deals where the customer is visited 4 times on average before winning the deal	400 visits
Results generated by the sales organization	
100 won deals at an average revenue of 75 KEUR/deal	7.5 MEUR
Gross profit at 40% margin	3.0 MEUR
Expenses sales people (10 pers.)	−1.0 MEUR
Earnings	**2.0** MEUR

Figure 3.1 Customer visits are used to secure customer loyalty and to drive new business deals, which creates revenue and leads to estimated earnings.

Create free capacity

There are two ways to create free capacity compared to the current way of operation, which will increase the productivity:

- **Increase quality.** Examples of doing this are to prioritize and approach customers more profitable to you, or to improve how you work with your customers, driving your business opportunities more successfully and winning a larger portion of them. If you increase the quality, the sales will increase as long as the work intensity (quantity) is constant.

- **Increase quantity.** In this case, it's a matter of making the sales organization work at a higher pace – having the sales people do more customer visits, driving more business opportunities, etc. If you increase the pace (quantity), the sales will increase as long as the quality of the execution of your deals are constant.

The company in the example from figure 3.1 could choose either direction in increasing their productivity. Having visited all "other customers" twice per year, the company can choose to re-prioritize this group such that less customers from the group are visited. This reduction in the number of customer visits would then free up capacity to drive new business. Furthermore, they can create *additional* capacity to drive new business by increasing the quantity (number of customer visits) the sales people do.

Affecting the income statement.

The free capacity that is created can then be reinvested in approaching new customers and driving business opportunities, or by reducing the number of sales people. The effect on the income statement will be increased revenue and lower costs, respectively.

- **Reinvest in approaching new customers.** Based on the example above, we can see that the company increases both their quality and quantity (figure 3.2). The free capacity is used to drive more business opportunities, and the company can win 60 % more deals and increase their revenue by 60 %, with all other parameters being constant

	Initial position	Using free capacity
Number of visits generated by the organization		
10 sales people making 160 visits per person and year	1,600 visits	
10 sales people making 200 visits per person and year:		2,000 visits
Number of visits consumed by the organization		
I: To secure customer loyalty		
50 major customers visited 4 times/year	200 visits	
200 other customers visited 2 times/year	400 visits	
50 major customers visited 4 times/year		200 visits
100 medium customers visited 2 times/year		200 visits
II: To drive business deals		
Participating in 300 deals where the customer is visited 2 times on average before losing the deal	600 visits	
Participating in 100 deals where the customer is visited 4 times on average before winning the deal	400 visits	
Participating in 480 deals where the customer is visited 2 times on average before losing the deal:		960 visits
Participating in 160 deals where the customer is visited 4 times on average before winning the deal:		640 visits
Results generated by the sales organization		
100 won deals at an average revenue of 75 KEUR/deal	7.5 MEUR	
160 won deals at an average revenue of 75 KEUR/deal		12.0 MEUR
Gross profit at 40% margin	3.0 MEUR	4.8 MEUR
Expenses 10 sales people	−1.0 MEUR	−1.0 MEUR
Earnings	**2.0 MEUR**	**3.8 MEUR**

Figure 3.2 The free capacity that is found is reinvested to drive new business opportunities, which will increase sales, revenues and earnings considerably.

- **Realize the savings.** The company can also use the free capacity to reduce the number of sales people. In this scenario, the company is more focused on reducing costs, and has little faith in their ability to win more business using the free capacity they have found. Then the question is how many sales people are needed, after the performance increase, to drive the same business volume as before? In figure 3.3 below, we see the number of sales people reduced by 30 % and the cost of sales reduced by 30 %.

	Initial position	Using free capacity
Number of visits generated by the organization		
10 sales people making 160 visits per person and year	1.600 visits	
7 sales people making 200 visits per person and year:		1.400 visits
Number of visits consumed by the organization		
I: To secure customer loyalty		
50 major customers visited 4 times/year	200 visits	
200 other customers visited 2 times/year	400 visits	
50 major customers visited 4 times/year		200 visits
100 medium customers visited 2 times/year		200 visits
II: To drive business deals		
Participating in 300 deals where the customer is visited 2 times on average before losing the deal	600 visits	
Participating in 100 deals where the customer is visited 4 times on average before winning the deal	400 visits	
Participating in 300 deals where the customer is visited 2 times on average before losing the deal		600 visits
Participating in 100 deals where the customer is visited 4 times on average before winning the deal		400 visits

Results generated by the sales organization		
100 won deals at an average revenue of 75 KEUR/deal	7.5 MEUR	
100 won deals at an average revenue of 75 KEUR/deal		7.5 MEUR
Gross profit at 40% margin	3.0 MEUR	3.0 MEUR
Expenses 10 and 7 sales people resp.	−1.0 MEUR	−0.7 MEUR
Earnings	**2.0 MEUR**	**2.3 MEUR**

Figure 3.3 In this case, the free capacity is used to reduce the number of sales people and the associated costs. Since the revenues are unchanged, the earnings are improved.

Relationship model

Figure 3.4 below, summarizes this chapter by showing the relationship between the income statement and changes in the performance of the sales force, and how this performance is influenced by the management of the sales force – both in qualitative and quantitative terms

In what areas you can improve the performance, and what tools that are available to management is what the next part of this book (chapters 4-12) is about.

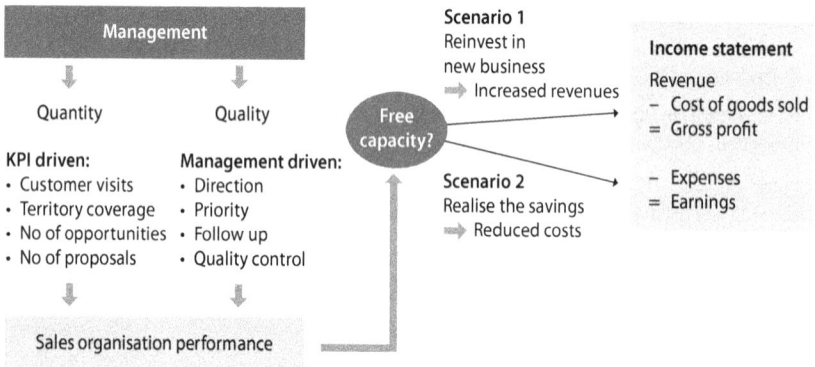

Figure 3.4 When the sales organization increases productivity, it will free capacity that can be used to improve results. Either by increasing revenue or by decreasing costs.

Summary

Sales organizations have a major influence on the income statement of the company. How to increase their performance and how this will affect the income statement can be analyzed in three steps; reviewing the current performance, detecting free capacity, and finally calculating the effect on the income statement.

The number of activities needed to protect current business and to drive new business is the basis for assessing the current performance. Capacity can be detected and freed by increasing the quality (how you work) or quantity (how many activities you do). The free capacity can be used to reinvest in driving new business or in savings, by reducing the sales force.

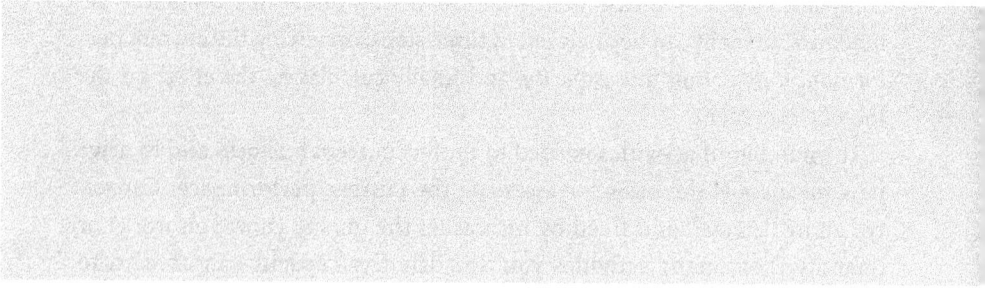

PART II

Model for managing sales organizations

CHAPTER 4

DIMENSION 1:
Territory management

Which customers a company is approaching with its offering is a natural starting point when organizing its sales force. Focusing the sales organization on the right type of customers and ensuring that they work these customers in a desirable way requires clarity from the company. Those who succeed well in this are characterized by:

- The company has created a clear picture for each sales person which customers (existing and potential) they are responsible for.
- The sales responsibility for each customer is clearly defined.
- There is a prioritization structure in place, used to identify the customers with greater importance and to where the priority affects how you work with these customers.
- There is a process for aligning sales territories, where work load and customer responsibilities between sales people are balanced, allowing the company to use their sales resources to maximize market potential.

Clear customer picture

In addition to segmenting the market into broad customer groups, the sales organization needs to identify the individual customers it is going to approach. If the company can name all the customers – even the potential ones – that a sales person is responsible for they have succeeded in creating a clear customer picture.

Segmentation

What customers, existing and potential, the company is approaching is a fundamental issue in marketing. Overall, the work consists of the following steps:

1. **What "mega markets" you choose to be present on.** Obviously, but not always expressed, is geographical region. "We are present in Western Europe, but not in North America or Africa", "We work in the Nordic countries" are examples of this.

2. **Segmentation of the market.** When segmenting the market, you divide it into parts where customers share some characteristics.[4] Basic segmentation, also called macro segmentation, is usually done based on geography, size and industry. Classifying customers based on this is normally sufficient; where you can identify the segments on the market you are most likely to succeed. If the macro segments would prove insufficient in dividing the market into relevant parts, micro segmentation could be used. Here the market is divided into different purchase behaviors of the customers.[5].

3. **Select target group.** Which segments of the market you choose to approach could be a combination of segmentation criteria, e.g. "Manufacturing companies (industry) with more than 200 employees (size), in the Greater Stockholm area (geography)".

4. **Identify the decision makers,** i.e. what roles at the customers are you approaching, e.g. "Production managers".

So far, the company has a good picture of which customers they generally approach. It is sufficient to satisfy the basic needs when targeting customers with a non-personal approach, such as advertising or direct marketing. Here is usually where the segmentation work ends for the marketing department, but for a sales organization a few more steps are required to get a fully functional model.

5. **Divide into sales territories.** Here the company decides how to split the target group between sales resources. What parts of the target

groups should be approached with sales people and what parts should be handled by other channels (tele-sales, contact centers, web shop, etc.)? The mechanisms for dividing into sales territories are usually the same as for macro segments, shown above. A sales person could be responsible for a geographical region, a specific industry, companies of a certain size, or a combination of all. You could also divide the target groups according to purchase behavior (micro segmentation). An example of this could be when using a contact center to handle all the straight-out procurement customers and their orders, instead of using sales people.

6. **The individual sales district.** The final step in this process is to list all the customers (existing and potential) that each sales person is responsible for. To name all these customers makes it easy for the sales people to contact customers without first having to search for the information. It also creates a good overview of the sales district, making it easier to assess its potential.

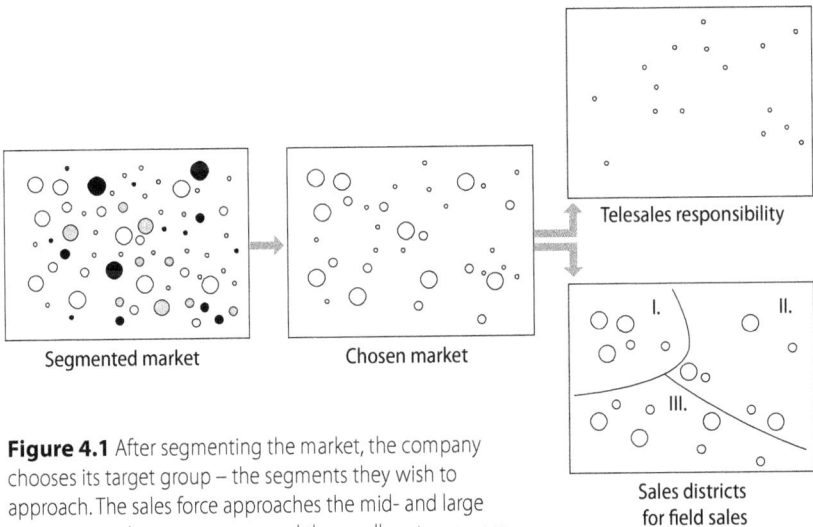

Segmented market   Chosen market

Telesales responsibility

I.   II.

III.

Sales districts
for field sales

Figure 4.1 After segmenting the market, the company chooses its target group – the segments they wish to approach. The sales force approaches the mid- and large customers in the target group, and the small customers are approached by telesales.

Named customers

To have a clear picture of the customer you are responsible for is a basic requirement for succeeding in a proactive sales role. It is difficult to follow up the progress on how you are approaching certain customers if this responsibility is unclear.

To create a clear picture the sales person needs the names of the customers in his or her districts. A sales district then becomes a list of names of existing and potential customers that the company expects the sales person to approach. Regardless of whether a sales district is based on geography, industry or size of companies, it is powerful to identify who those customers are by name. The benefit of this is that the company has made their expectations clear and steers the sales people to the right customers. The sales people don't have to spend time on searching and making their own interpretations on what the right target group is. In doing this, the company will, at the same time, get a list of the size and potential of the districts.

Most sales organizations will list and name *existing* customers to be divided between the sales people. However, this is rarely done for *potential* customers. To obtain these names are certainly more difficult, but not as demanding as one might believe. Having once defined the target group it is fairly straightforward to generate a list with potential customer names from one of the many suppliers of address databases.

Clear responsibility

The most common scenario is that one dedicated sales person has the sole responsibility for a customer. But there are two instances where you need to clarify the sales responsibility.

- When more than one person is selling to the customer
- When other roles than sales people sell to the customer

More than one sales person working the same customer

To have more than one sales person working the same customer is quite common when you sell to very large customers – usually called Key Accounts. To clarify the roles and responsibilities of the sales people sharing the same customer is therefore a good idea. The sales responsibility can be defined by:

- **Who is responsible for which department at the customer.** Sometimes the different departments could be regarded as companies within the company.
- **Who is responsible for what part of the company's offer to the customer.** If the company has a complex offer to the customer, this may require a specialized sales force for different parts of the offer.
- **Who is overall responsible for the customer.** It's not always necessary to have someone appointed as the overall responsible sales person, but it's quite common when you need central contacts to negotiate and follow up central agreements.

If you don't clarify the areas of responsibility, you risk ending up in a situation where different sales people approach the same customer contact with the same offer. Apart from the unnecessary extra cost this double approach leads to, it will most likely be regarded as unprofessional by the customer and it will lead to internal conflict in the sales force.

Other roles than sales people selling

It's also important to clarify the responsibility from another aspect. There are many roles within a company that may have a sales responsibility even though they are not called sales people. Consultant, project manager, advisor or service engineer could be examples of such roles.

If the person responsible for sales also has other roles, it is important to clarify the sales responsibility:

- For which customers are they responsible.
- What are their sales targets (we will cover targets in chapter 5).

Selling is not an easy task. If the expectations are unclear, it is easy to put aside the sales task and focus on other tasks, which will cause sales to suffer.

Companies will sometimes call their sales people by a different name for cosmetic reasons, because there is skepticism to the sales title in the company or among its customers. There are examples of industries where the sales title has been replaced by other titles entirely. In these cases, it would of course be strange to choose different titles.

However, in general we find that successful companies with focus on personal sales emphasize and take pride in the sales role, which is also reflected in the titles they use.

Prioritizing customers

Some customers are more important than others. It is reasonable that a customer with the potential to generate 10 MEUR is more important than a customer with a potential to generate only 1 MEUR. A good tool to help sales organizations focus on their most important customers is by classifying the customers in some order of priority. A-B-C, Gold-Silver-Bronze, Prio-1, Prio-2, Prio-3 are examples of such classifications. There has to be some practical implication of the classification, otherwise there is no point in doing it. Here is what it may look like, depending on whom the company sells to:

Priority examples of end customers

- A-customers, with a potential to buy for more than 1 MEUR, will be visited by field sales at least once a quarter.

- B-customers, with a potential to buy for more than 100 KEUR, will be visited by field sales at least twice a year.

- C-customers, with a potential for less than 100 KEUR in purchases, will not be approached by field sales, but tele-sales will contact them twice per year.

Priority examples of resellers (partners)

- Gold partners, are certified on our products, buy for more than 10 MEUR per year, have 25% discount on list price and has the right to sign service agreements with the end customer. We follow up our Gold partners 4 times per year.

- Silver partners, are not certified but buy for more than 10 MEUR per year, have 20% discount on list price. We follow up our Silver partners 2 times per year.

- Bronze partners, buying for 1-10 MEUR – irrespective of certification, have 10% discount on list price. We follow up our Bronze partners 1 time per year.

Note that the classification – apart from the number of follow-up visits – also has consequences in the commercial terms with the reseller (partner).

Who prioritizes

Which customers that are the most important to the company – and the ones you first and foremost would like to approach – is a strategic question, and therefore a task for the management.

It is, however, wise to involve the sales people in the classification process. They possess the local market knowledge from their sales territories and could help refine the priorities further. In addition, it helps to more firmly establish the target market for each sales person.

The basis for priority

The type of customers that should be prioritized depends on what is important to the company. It doesn't always have to be the largest customers from a purchasing volume. It could just as well be the customers that are the most profitable ones, or the ones that add most value to the company's products, etc.

Another important aspect in setting priorities is to look at the *potential* of the customers. If you only consider the historical purchase volumes, you might miss the customers that have a small purchase volume from you but are buying substantial volumes from the competitors. These customers are likely to represent a good potential, which should be reflected in the priority.

Sometimes you are faced with the loyalty concept as a complementing dimension for making priorities. As an example, a large customer with a high loyalty to your company would be called A1, and a medium sized company with low level of loyalty would be called B3. The need for the loyalty aspect is questionable in terms of making priorities. Firstly, because there is no clear relation between loyalty and profitability[6]. Secondly, the question of loyalty introduces an unnecessary complexity in the priority classification, which is likely to result in it not being used. If you let your classification be based on potential sales, it should be sufficient to direct the sales force to the right type of customers

A final comment concerning priorities: The larger the territories the sales people should cover, the more important it becomes to make priorities. The sales person may not even be able to cover the district fully during the year, making it more important for the company to steer the sales resources so that at least the most important customers are being approached.

Prioritizing customers – a profitable approach for the manufacturing company

The company had a long and successful history of selling tools to the manufacturing industry. Over the decades they had built a sales force that with a high degree of autonomy approached and served the customer base. Since a couple of years, the successful trend had been broken, as the customers started moving their production facilities to Asia. Sales were declining, putting pressure on profitability. An analysis of their revenues revealed a long tail of small customers.

In the diagram below, you see a bar for each customer in a declining order, where the biggest customer buys for more than one million EUR down to the smallest of the 235 customers buying for virtually nothing. Half of the customers represented only 2 % of the revenues, which is indicated by the full line showing accumulated sales for the customers in a declining order.

The profitability from the smaller customers was so low it was hard to justify sending a sales person to visit them. Already after a meeting or two the cost for the sales meetings would exceed the gross profit from a potential order. The company realized that, in order to improve profitability, they needed to give clearer directions to their sales people on what customers to approach. It led to the following classification of customers:

1. The customers with the greatest potential were to be protected. It was decided that the responsible sales person should visit these at least once a quarter. The purpose was partly to follow-up on product and delivery quality, but mainly to detect new business opportunities and to try to keep the competition out.

2. Medium sized customers were also to be handled by the sales people, who were responsible for finding and driving business opportunities among these. There were no formal requirements for how often these should be visited by the sales people. The business opportunities they were driving among these customers dictated the number of visits they received.

3. The smallest customers, who also didn't have the potential to become bigger, were transferred to local distributors. The distributor channel became responsible for selling and servicing the small customer segment.

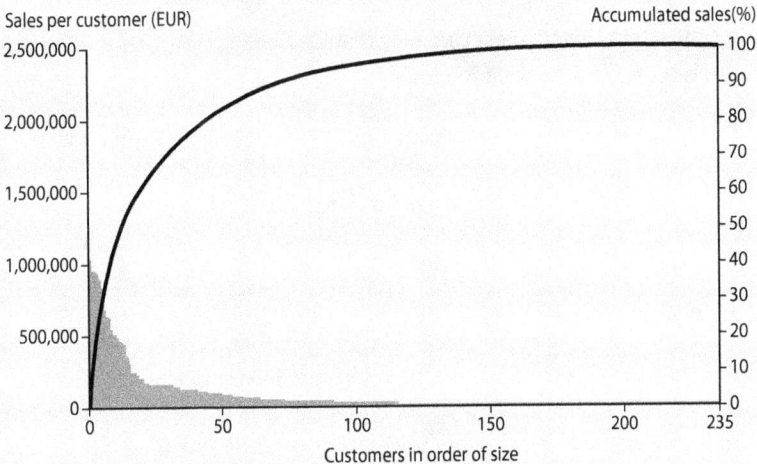

Figure 4.2 The manufacturing company´s customers in declining order and accumulated sales.

Should the priority classification be open to the customers?

If you choose to be open with the priority classification, you have a tool by which you can develop the customer relationship. A high priority customer will feel prioritized, not only in how the supplier acts but also emotionally, in the sense of recognition.

When selling through resellers, distributors and other channel partners it is quite common with open priority classifications, where the different classes also have different commercial terms. Priority classes could also be related to more than just purchasing volumes of the reseller. Examples include: product training of the reseller's personnel, the reseller's commitment to stocking the product, agreeing to not carry the competitors' products, etc.

In general, if you choose to be open about the classification, you need to be consistent and keep to the rules of the classification. If you deviate and allow exceptions from the rules to some partners, others are likely to feel disfavored. Consistency is especially important when establishing the rules and moving away from a "wheeling-and-dealing" handling of a partner network (i.e. where you continuously give special treatments, negotiate and adapt to every single situation).

The document management company that created clear rules for their partner program

The Japanese document management company had just acquired a competitor and on the new CEO's agenda was to merge the two partner networks, one that had been managed in a regulated way and the other that had been handled in an informal way. They set up a program with Gold, Silver, and Bronze partners. The Gold partners received high discounts in return for high purchasing volumes. The Silver partners received less discounts and a lower purchase requirement. The Bronze partners had no purchase requirements and therefore the lowest discounts. The program was thoroughly prepared and was well received when presented to the partners. Only two partners were not content and they had strong objections. One was the biggest reseller from the informal network, who couldn't accept that they no longer had any special treatment. They even suggested that there should be a "Platinum" category, where they should be the only qualified partner.

The other dissatisfied partner was a newly founded company that believed they should be Gold partners based on their management's previous merits from the industry. "We have fifteen years' experience from the industry, of course we should be Gold partners." The new CEO and his team stood firm and defended the new program. When implemented, the new program was a big success in general and the only negative effect was a marginally lower purchase volume from the self-defined "Platinum" partner.

Balancing sales territories

As mentioned in the introduction of this book – when we talk about sales person's territory, we mean those customer (existing and potential) that sales person is responsible for. These customers typically belong to a certain geographical area or a certain industry.

Balancing sales territories means that you allocate customers so you even out the workload between sales people. It is not about achieving perfect fairness between sales people, but rather to ensure that the company has the capacity to approach the most important customers. Some sales people may not have time to cover all their key customers, while others don't have enough potential to work with. For the company, balancing is simply a matter of maximizing their sales potential.

Imbalance is often detected when companies recruit new sales people. Among the old, experienced sales people there could be a reluctance to let go of any customers, leaving the new sales people with the customers no one else wanted. This reluctance to let go of customers sometimes has its root in how the sales people are compensated (more about that in chapter 5). Sometimes it is based on the incorrect assumption that the customer "belongs" to old sales person. This of course is absurd – the customer belongs to the company!

It is good practice for the company to review and align the sales territories, at least annually, when sales budgets are decided. There are, however, other methods to handle the issue, as you can see in the example below.

Dynamic customer allocation

The media company published a free newspaper that was financed through advertising sales. A key to their success was their ability to attract both small local enterprises as well as big national advertisers, such as realty agencies.

During a job interview the new sales person enquired: "How do I know I will get a reasonable sales district if I come over to you? Old sales people rarely let go of any customers, even though they don't have time to work them all."

The sales manager explained that all sales people have a list where all their customers were named.

"You will get a list like that when you begin. To reduce the risk of forgetting any customer, we have introduced the following rule: If the responsible sales person has not been in contact with the customer for six months, any sales person is allowed to take over the responsibility. In the CRM system you can see what customers are available, and after I formally approve it the customer is transferred. In that way you can always expand your list."

With this dynamic allocation process the media company ensured that the most interesting customers always were covered. Another positive effect was that a sales person could specialize in a certain segment by monitoring and taking over neglected customers, similar to the ones he had experience from.

Territory coverage

Territory coverage is a way to verify how well balanced the sales districts are, i.e. how many customers the sales person has covered during a certain period.

If the sales person has a problem covering his district – especially the most important customers – the company should consider transferring his customers to a colleague with better capacity. Alternatively, if free capacity does not exist anywhere in the sales force, the company needs to recruit more sales people or introduce a tougher priority where less attention is paid to customers of lower importance. To calculate the capacity needed to work the customer base, we refer to chapter 10.

The Fast Moving Consumables company had full control of their territory coverage

The company approached the major retail chains with its sales force. Each sales person had a list of all the retailers in their district, who were to be visited during every campaign cycle. The sales territories were designed so that each sales person, with appropriate planning, could visit all customers in his territory. The customer list was regularly reviewed, where they made sure that all the major outlets were listed and they didn't miss any newly established outlets. This review was done with the sales manager, the sales person and the key account manager for the outlet chain, who provided the list.

The visits were made during the campaign cycles, which lasted for approximately six weeks. During the year they had a number of different campaigns; e.g. launching new products. The sales person's responsibility was to inform customers about the products, assist in merchandising them and to secure orders from the retailers.

The company measured how many visits were made, and to which retailer, during every campaign cycle. By doing this they ensured that the sales people really covered their districts as planned.

Summary

Allocating responsibilities for potential and existing customers to different sales people is important for outbound sales to be effective. A first step is a segmentation of the market from which the target group is selected for the sales force to approach. The sales people need a clear picture of the customers they are expected to approach and providing them with a list of company names and contacts – for both existing and potential customers – is a great help in achieving that.

In a lot of cases, roles other than sales people are involved in the customer contacts. If these roles also have a responsibility to generate sales this should be clearly stated and a target needs to be formulated.

On top of allocating customers to different sales people, there is also a need to help them prioritize their approach. Customers that are more profitable and represent higher purchase volumes should have a higher priority than others. An important aspect when setting priorities is to consider potential revenues and not only historical purchases.

Sales management should regularly review how well the sales people are covering their districts, and reallocate customers where needed so that the company has the capacity to approach the most interesting customers.

CHAPTER 5

DIMENSION 2:
Target setting, follow-up & reward

How you target and follow-up sales people is a discipline consisting of many parts. In general, those who are successful in this dimension have the following in place:

- The targets are individual
- Follow-up on results is frequent
- Situational targets are used for stimulating temporary sales efforts
- If performance-based salaries are used, they should be easy to understand and stimulate the desired behavior among the sales people

Individual targets

Breaking down targets to an individual level is an effective strategy when managing sales people because it is more likely that the individual will assume the responsibility and accountability for the target. However, in some cases it may be difficult to formulate individual targets, and you must rely on group targets. In these circumstances the guiding principle should be that the targets should be as close to the individual as possible, so it is possible for the sales person to influence the outcome. If a person only has a marginal impact on the results, a lot of the motivation in working towards that target is lost.

Whether it is an individual or a group target, it is crucial for management to communicate the target to the individuals and to get confirmation that the target is understood. A written target document, signed by both the sales person and manager by the beginning of each budget period, is an excellent tool to achieve this.

When targeting sales people there are some points worth noting, which also should be reflected in the target document.

- That you have few targets.

- That the targets are constructed in a SMART way (SMART being an acronym for Specific, Measurable, Achievable, Relevant and Time-bound).

- That you specify which performance areas, the Key Performance Indicators (KPI), you measure and what the targets are for the individual.

Number of targets

The most common target for sales people is of course their sales target. This goal is usually expressed in revenue, but gross profit is becoming an increasingly common metric – especially in industries where sales margins are small.

In addition to sales targets it's becoming more frequent for sales people to have targets in other areas. On top of the individual sales target there is usually a group target for the sales team or the company, as well as other parameters such as customer satisfaction.[7]

Sometimes, balanced scorecards are used to set targets in areas which are difficult to measure financially.

Balanced Scorecards

Balanced Scorecards[8] is a method for measuring that was introduced 1992 by Robert S. Kaplan and David P. Norton. The method has its origin in the notion that financial measurements should not be the only measurements used for measuring and managing an organization. To give a balanced view of the business, they believed that a total of 15-20 measures in four areas, perspectives, were needed. The four perspectives are:

- Financial perspective (financial position, profitability)

- Customer perspective (customer satisfaction, market share)

- Learning and Development perspective (innovation intensity, new products share of sales)

- Internal processes (lead times, quality)

When balanced scorecards are used in a sales organization, they could address such areas as customer satisfaction, market share, and even whether or not the sales people are sufficiently trained on the company's products.

When using several targets, you should bear in mind that the more targets you add, the less focus each target will receive – and managing by these targets will become less effective. It's therefore recommendable to use as few targets as possible. The danger in using balanced scorecards in sales organizations is that they contain too many parameters, which works against the simplicity.

Target document 2016				
Area	**Target**	**Method for measuring**	**Result**	**%**
Annual revenue for your team	15.6 MEUR	Revenues according to income statement		
Earnings for your team	430 KEUR	EBITDA, income statement		
Customer satisfaction for your customers	> 3.7	Score according to customer survey in quarter 4		
Market share	> 18 %	No. of sold units according to Industry survey during quarter 3		
Sales people trained on new methodology	100 %	Conducted before quarter 3. Verified by HR		
Employee satisfaction	> 3.5	Score according to employee survey in quarter 4		

Figure 5.1 Example of a balanced scorecard for a sales manager.

Except for the mathematical effect, where more targets mean less focus on each target, there is another reason to have fewer targets. As human beings we can only keep a limited number of things in our mind at the same time, this is supported by psychological research. The number of things we can keep in mind is limited by the capacity of the working memory, which is limited to three or four things.[9] (Note that we sometimes can overcome this limitation by grouping the information. Well-designed balanced scorecards take this into consideration.)

Successful managers of sales organizations realize the value of few targets. They choose to focus on few targets, even though the company has many more parameters on their scorecard.

SMART construction of targets

Irrespective of what type of targets you plan to use in the sales organization, the SMART-concept[10] is very useful when formulating targets. The SMART acronym stands for:

- **Specific.** A target is specific when it is clearly defined and does not allow for any ambiguity or alternative interpretations. Individual revenue targets for sales people, where they are expected to sell for X EUR per year to their customer base, are examples of specific targets.

- **Measurable.** That you are able to measure the target means that it is not based on arbitrary assessment. Measurability is vital when you follow how well the results develop in relation to the target over time. Sometimes you also need to specify from which source you intend to measure. Do you, for example, measure sales from the order book or from invoiced revenue? And if you measure customer satisfaction, how do you measure it?

- **Achievable.** This term means that the targets should be both realistic and challenging. Challenging because we want the sales people to put in some effort in finding new opportunities, but the targets also need be reachable when putting in the extra effort. You want sales people to assume responsibility for their targets. – If the targets are unrealistic, you will lose that motivational effect. At the same time, you risk losing the motivational effect if the targets are too easy to reach. Why bother trying when you reach the targets anyway?

- **Relevant.** Relevant targets measure the right things – what you want the sales people to achieve. Do you want them to sell as many products as possible, do you want them to maximize the gross profit or do you want them to generate as much revenue as possible to new customers? Unfortunately, it is not unusual for companies to have a mismatch between how they target sales people and what the vital goals for the company are. One example is when sales people have revenue-based targets (and give generous discounts to achieve this revenue), while the company has tight margins and aim for higher profitability. Another example is when sales people are measured on all sales, where the dominating portion comes from existing customers, despite the company's urgent need for new customers.

- **Time-bound.** To have a final date by which the target should be met is rarely a problem in sales organizations. Sales budgets are per definition bound in time to year, quarter or month. If you have other type of targets it is therefore important to specify by when they should be achieved.

SMART analysis by the French subsidiary

The French subsidiary was under pressure to improve the profitability. The company's products were sold to the manufacturing industry and they had managed and targeted the sales force in the same way for many years.

The French country manager had the annual budget process ahead of her, and she was contemplating different approaches for improved profitability, not just cost cutting.

She had experience from several industries and decided to review whether the targets for the sales organizations were set properly.

After having analyzed them with the help of SMART, she concluded that they were both specific and measurable. Each sales person was measured on the invoiced value to their customers, which could easily be retrieved from the income statement and the accounts receivable. The targets were also formulated as annual targets, so the time-bound aspect was not a problem either. What made her wonder was whether the targets were achievable and relevant.

- **Achievable.** The country manager concluded that the targets were not really achievable. Traditionally they had been set at very high levels since they wanted the sales people to work extremely hard to reach them. In practice the sales people felt that the targets didn't mean anything since they were too unrealistic. "No one achieves them anyway" was a common response. Besides losing the motivational effect in working towards a target, the target levels became a source of irritation in the sales force

- **Relevant.** The manager became self-critical when she saw how they had targeted the sales people incorrectly and how easy it was to fix it. We should've corrected this a long time ago, she thought. Throughout the years the sales people had been measured on revenue. During the last couple of years, they were facing considerably lower gross margins and they were struggling with their profitability. Since the sales people were not measured on gross margin they were not particularly concerned about it, and it was quite common they gave generous discounts in order to win business, which hurt the profitability even harder.

Based on the analysis, the company redesigned their targets. They created targets so they would be realistic but not too easy to reach, with the aim that between 70% and 90% of the sales people should reach them. In addition, they changed the basis for how they measured sales. Instead of having revenue targets they started to measure the gross profit the sales people generated.

KPIs

In addition to measuring results, sales organizations frequently measure the performance of their sales people in other ways. These performance measures could be part of the balanced scorecards mentioned previously, or they may appear separately.

These performance measures are usually called KPIs – Key Performance

Indicators. By measuring these, the company can better predict what the results will be later.

KPIs are sometimes called activity targets since you usually measure different activities from the company's sales process. Examples of KPIs could be number of qualified business opportunities, number of proposals, or the value of all proposals sent.

A generic measure that suits most field sales organizations is the number of customer visits. It gives an indication whether the sales person has enough pace in order cover his district and to drive the number of deals needed to reach his budget.

In the same way where you want to have as few targets as possible, the same applies to KPIs. The fewer you have, the more focus on them. They are called "key" for a reason.

KPI for the MedTech Company

The MedTech Company sold blood analysis equipment to private doctor's offices on the German market. In a project when auditing the sales organization, they realized they didn't have any performance measures, only historical sales results. "We look too much in the rear view mirror, and not on the road ahead" the country manager sighed. He sat down together with one of the more successful sales people to discuss their sales process and how they could find relevant performance measures.

"I always offer the customer the trial period before deciding to buy, which I think everyone should do", the sales person said. What she referred to was the possibility for the sales people to offer a free trial period of a month, after having presented the product. It sped up the decision process and a majority of the customers decided to purchase the equipment.

The company started measuring how many of the products on trial were converted to sales and found that almost 75% of the customers kept their equipment. This trial step was then incorporated in their sales process and selected as a KPI. Whatever was on trial in a month would be converted to sales in 75% of the cases the next month. They had created an excellent ground for predicting their revenues and to target and drive their sales force.

Follow-up

The continuous follow-up of sales people's performance in relation to their targets is vital in making them assume responsibility for their targets and results. It is also a central part of creating motivation and commitment in sales. The follow-up is a way to ensure that sales people see the results of their work, even if the end results may lie in the future. To see the results of one's work has proven an important factor for high productivity.

The case of Legos – meaningful conditions

Research supporting this is for example "The case of Legos". Subjects in an experiment were tasked to assemble a certain Lego Bionicle model according to instructions. The subjects were paid 2.0 USD for the first model, 1.89 USD (0.11 USD less) for the second model, and so on. For the 20th assembled model and thereafter 0.02 USD was paid. Each subject only had one decision to make – when to stop assembling models. Then they were paid and the experiment was over.

The subjects were divided into two groups. In the group "Meaningful condition" they subjects were to place the assembled model on the table in front of them and they were given a new box with parts to build. As they kept working the table was filled with assembled models

In the other group, "Sisyphus condition", there were only two boxes of the Bionicle model. After the subject completed the first Bionicle and began working on the second, the experimenter would disassemble the first Bionicle into pieces and place the pieces back into the box.

Hence, the number of assembled models didn't accumulate, since they were constantly rebuilt by the subject and disassembled by the experimenter.

This was the only difference between the two conditions. Furthermore, all the Bionicles were identical, so the "Meaningful condition" did not provide more variety than the "Sisyphus" one.

The result of the experiment showed that the group "Meaningful condition" built significantly more Bionicle models than the "Sisyphus group", on average 10.6 models (earned 14.40 USD) versus 7.2 models (11.52 USD).

Meaningful conditions where you could see the result of your work gave a significantly higher productivity.[11]

When a company sets up the follow-up procedures they need to decide

- The format for the follow-up,
- The frequency of the follow-up, and
- That you consistently follow up on all sales people.

Format

Continuously sending out the results to the sales person (or making it available in some IT system) is of course a good foundation for giving feedback on results, but it is not enough if you want to create commitment and motivation.

The follow-up needs to be based on human interaction, meaning that the manager and the sales person go through and discuss the results. If there is a negative deviation compared to the plan, you need to understand why and what needs to be done in order to close that gap.

Ideally, this follow-up is done in a one-to-one meeting, where you can bring up difficult issues and give candid feedback. In a group meeting where the entire sales group participate, that opportunity is lost.

Frequency

The follow-up allows the manger to check if the results of the sales people are developing according to plan, and to decide together with the sales people if corrective actions are necessary. The earlier you put in corrective actions, the more likely they will influence the end results. Therefore, the time span shouldn't be too long before following up on the results of the sales people. How often you should do the follow-ups depends on the time frame of the target. A rule of thumb could be the following:

- If you have an annual target (which is the most common in sales forces), you should do monthly follow-ups.
- If you have monthly targets, you should have weekly follow-ups.
- If you have weekly targets, you should have daily follow-ups.

Consistency

It is vital that you are consistent when following up the sales people, which mean you follow up *all* sales people at *all* the follow-up opportunities. Not only when sales people fall behind in their results. If follow-up only happens as a consequence of low performance, it will be perceived as something negative.

By consistently doing follow-ups with all, you can discuss with and encourage everyone to improve their results, not only the small group which has fallen behind.

Situational targets

During the year you may experience that the annual sales target is insufficient for managing specific situations and stimulating certain behaviors. In these situations, you can complement them by setting temporary, short-term targets. These targets are called situational targets, and they can be introduced during the year whenever there is need for encouraging sales in a certain area.

Situational targets can be used for encouraging sales on a specific product or service. They could for example be used when introducing new products, that will get a better start when they are targeted and followed up specifically. The company can also choose to use the performance-based part of the salary to reinforce the situational target:

- The performance-based part of the salary will be paid only under the condition that a certain volume of the new product has been sold.
- Sales of the new product will be rewarded more favorably than the other products.

The situational targets could also be used to drive certain behavior and activities; i.e. to follow up customer leads from an exhibition.

When following up situational targets it is often done in a format where sales people compete against each other. In the examples above it could be who sold most of the new products or who was the fastest one to follow up the leads from the exhibition. The winner will be recognized, of course, and sometimes also a reward.

If you want to get full effect from the situational targets it is – just as it is with normal targets – important to have a continuous follow-up of the sales people, so they can see how they are in relation to their targets and to each other.

Two sales competitions at the Fast Moving Consumables Company

The FMC Company had product managers who were responsible for designing the campaigns aimed at consumers shopping in the big retail chains.

A central part for succeeding with the campaigns was how well they were received by the company's sales force, which was a common resource for the product mangers to reach the retailers. To make it attractive for the sales people to work with their products the two product managers, Cecilia and Amanda, each designed a sales competition. Even though it was not formulated it was understood that their campaigns were to compete.

Cecilia had been careful in using her budgeted funds so far during the year and decided to use a substantial part of it for this campaign. At the start of the campaign she presented a prestigious and expensive prize the winning sales person was to receive. When the campaign was over she presented the winner and handed over the prize.

Amanda didn't have much budget left and the prizes were mostly symbolic and humorous. Instead she spent time every week during the two-month campaign cycle to inform the sales people who was leading and how they were doing in relation to each other. Not only did she send out ranking lists, she also called sales people to pep them. The product manager that succeeded most in her campaign was Amanda. Through the constant feedback in sending out results and pepping the sales people she appealed to their competitive side. That the prizes were not as valuable turned out to be less important.

Performance-based salary

Performance-based salary means the sales people have a variable part of their salary linked to their sales performance.

Do performance-based salaries work?

To have parts of salary based on sales results is quite common in sales organizations. In a survey on the Swedish market from 2008, we found that 80% of sales organizations have a performance-based salary in some shape or form.[12] Even though it is common occurrence it is often subject to discussion in many companies: Are performance-based salaries driving sales or are they, on the contrary, negative? Do they stimulate the sales people to perform or will they lead to worry and focus on private earnings rather than long-term customer benefits?

When the work content involves a high degree of creativity and problem solving, money is a questionable motivational tool as research has shown it has counterproductive effect in people trying to solve complex tasks. In tests it has been shown that groups that were offered money to solve a problem in as short period of time as possible, performed worse. In addition, the more they were offered, the worse they performed compared to the groups that were offered nothing at all.[13]

Performance based salaries in the right way

Performance-based salaries could be an effective way of reinforcing desirable behavior and driving better results. However, it requires you to think through the structure of what is being rewarded and it also requires fundamental pre-requisites to be in place, for example realistic targets and reasonable sales potential in all the sales districts.

The reinforcing effect of the performance-based salaries works both ways. It's an excellent tool for driving results when companies have thought through the programs and have created sound conditions for them to work in. When the programs haven't been thought through, they will lead to internal focus and discord.

Programs for performance-based salaries do not compensate for any structural problems – they reinforce them.

When designing a program, you should take the following into account:

- That they reward the right behavior.
- That they are easy to understand.
- That the individual can influence the outcome.
- That the reward is paid close in time.

Rewarding the right behavior

In the previously mentioned survey we did on the Swedish market 2008, we found that only a third of all companies that had performance-based salaries were satisfied with how they were working. The main explanation for this was that they didn't believe their programs were driving sales in the way they wanted. They didn't feel they were rewarding the right type of behavior in the sales force.[14]

How can you ensure that you reward the right type of behavior? Here are some aspects to consider:

- **Rewarding the right thing.** Are the rewards to the sales people in line with what you, as a company, want to achieve? It might sound obvious, but the fact is that it's quite common you'll find that the performance-based systems are out of line: Companies who reward their sales people on sales revenue even though it is profitability and gross profit that are important. Or companies rewarding on profit margin, even though they are trying to drive volume. There are also companies rewarding their sales people on activities, such as customer visits, and not results. Once again – what are they trying to achieve? If it's results, then you should reward results, not customer visits. Of course, it is important to stimulate sales people to do many customer visits, but that should be done through follow-up and coaching, not at the expense of focusing on results.

- **Avoid constricting systems.** The design of some performance-based systems may encourage the sales people to stop selling in certain situations, which is a highly undesirable behavior. This can happen when a sales person reaches the maximum limit for what is being paid, and where incremental sales will not be rewarded. Then there is a risk the sales person will postpone the sale to the next period, when calculating the performance-based rewards starts from scratch again.

It's understandable to have these maximum limits, since companies want to ensure that the variable compensations don't get out of control. But the maximum levels need to be at a high level so a sales person does not risk reaching it.

Another variation of a constricting system is when sales people postpone a sale to the next period when they risk not reaching the minimum level for when variable compensation is paid. For the sales person it becomes better to postpone the sale to the next period since it will improve the chances of reaching the minimum target in that period.

- **Avoid lock-in effects.** Previously (in chapter 4) we discussed the importance of balancing the workload between sales people to maximize the sales potential. Unfortunately, some designs in performance-based salaries lead to lock-in effects preventing a better balancing of sales districts. If a sales person's variable pay is based on a commission of what the customers buy for, they are reluctant to let go of any customer, since it will reduce their pay.

The performance-based salaries impeded the growth of the staffing agency

The staffing agency historically had seen a very strong growth since it started. They pointed out the commission-based salaries in the sales force as a strong contributing factor to the success, where sales people were generously rewarded for winning business with the large corporations.

The growth slowed down after a couple of years, even though there was still a lot of business to be won at the large corporations. The staffing agency started to recruit more sales people to address the untapped potential. However, the old sales people didn't want to let go of any interesting customers, even though they didn't have the capacity to cover them. They didn't want to miss any potential commission. "Do you want to take away our salaries when we are the ones who have developed the market for the company?"

The company was unable to change the territorial mind-set of the sales people and they failed in their further expansion. In addition, the turn-over of new sales people was very high, which also drove up expenses. "Why should I have to work on the customers no one else wants?" was a comment that was frequently heard among new sales people.

Easy to understand

If you want to create commitment and drive the right type of behavior the performance-based salaries need to be easy to understand for the sales people.

To avoid unnecessary complexity, we recommend you have few reward parameters and that simple mathematics can be used when calculating the variable pay.

- **Few parameters.** If you have too many reward parameters, it will be more difficult for the sales people to get an overview. Furthermore, the more parameters you have the lower importance each parameter will have. A major reason for having too many parameters is that companies are overambitious in trying to address every aspect of being a sales person. The usage of balanced scorecards in conjunction with rewards has unfortunately contributed to this.

- **Simple mathematics.** How you calculate the variable pay should be simple. For sales people to trust the system they should easily be able to verify the variable part themselves. If it becomes too difficult some sales people will give up – "it will be what it will be" – and others will spend a disproportional amount of time to figure out what their pay will be.

Influencing the outcome

Whatever the basis for reward, the sales person should be able to influence the outcome. The better the individual's ability to influence the outcome, the more effective it is a basis for reward.

This means that it is more effective to base a reward on revenue (or gross margin) than it is on net profit because the sales person has little influence over the allocated costs that are deducted before arriving at a net profit. In one case we have even seen sales people being penalized for credit losses. Of course, if it is part of the sales person's responsibility to make credit assessments on their customers, this measure could be understood. (Then the question would rather be why they don't use a more professional credit assessment process).

The ability to influence the outcome also means that rewards that are based on individual results are more effective than group results.

Close in time

To get a strong connection between the performance and what is being paid for the performance, you should reward the sales person as close as possible to when they win the business.

One aspect of this is how early you measure sales. Is it when the customer places the order? Or is it when you invoice the order? Or is it later, when the customer has paid?

Between order and payment it could be several months, depending on what industry you are in. The longer this time is, the more risk the company is exposed to. What happens if the order is cancelled, or what happens if the customer doesn't pay? This risk is a counterbalance to paying the variable parts of the salary early, and the company needs to consider this when deciding how close to the order they dare to pay. If they lose almost no business between the time of order and customer payment, it is easier to decide for an early payment of the performance-based part of the salary.

Another aspect of "close in time" is how often you pay this variable part of the salary. Ideally you should have a high frequency in the payments to reinforce the connection between payment and performance. If you choose to measure sales already at the order point some of that reinforcement will be lost if you only have payments once a year.

Annual payments are less motivating than those that are paid every quarter, or ideally, every month. The highest payment frequency we have seen is in an advertising sales company which paid the performance-based parts every Friday.

Summary

Target setting and follow-ups are central elements when managing a sales organization. Individual targets and follow-ups are more effective than group targets, and to have fewer targets as opposed to many is preferred based on psychological research. A good model to formulate targets is through "SMART", which means that goals should be Specific, Measurable, Achievable, Relevant and Time-bound.

It's a good practice to also measure other areas than financial results. Key Performance Indicators (KPI), is a term where you measure activities, (i.e. number of customer contacts, to better predict future results).

To follow-up on results and to see how they are progressing has a strong motivational effect. The follow-up should be done in formalized way and preferably in a "one-to-one" between sales person and the manager.

Situational, short-term targets could be used to complement the usual (often annual) sales targets. This could for example be used for putting focus on newly launched products.

Performance-based salaries are common in sales organizations. They will reinforce a desired behavior, if used correctly. They could also have negative effects if not handled properly. To work well these reward systems need to be easy to understand, the individuals need to be able to influence the results, and the salary payments of the variable part should be frequent and as close to the performance as possible.

CHAPTER 6

DIMENSION 3:
Visualizing the performance

Successful companies continuously visualize how their sales people are performing, which is an important part of the feedback to the sales people. In this chapter, we will cover the following aspects of visualization:

- Visualizing of results
- Visualizing of activities
- Recipients and availability
- Frequency of what is being visualized
- Formats for visualization

In the world of sports, it is the norm to have ranking lists and scoreboards, which are updated continuously. Successful companies use the same tools to create interest and motivation in sales, which figure 6.1 is an example of.

Feedback on performance is critical for executing the work tasks in a motivating way, according to Hackman and his colleagues[15].

Results Year-to-date	Sales	Budget	Performance
Anne	8,300	6,900	120 %
Robert	7,850	6,900	114 %
David	10,120	9,400	108 %
Marie	7,400	6,900	107 %
Christian	9,340	9,400	99 %
Catherine	8,650	9,400	92 %
Erica	5,200	6,900	75 %
Roland	5,600	9,400	60 %

Figure 6.1 Scoreboard for the sales department with the highest ranked sales person in the top and the rest of the sales people in descending order.

Visualization of results

The content of what is presented could either be based on results (for example, how much the sales people have sold for) or on activities (how many important activities the sales people have completed).

When presenting results, it should be easy and intuitive for the recipients of the information to understand how each sales person is performing. By presenting in a ranking list format, it is quickly understood which sales people perform the best.

Being at the top of the scoreboard is a way to recognize the highest performing sales people, and a motivational factor for the other sales people to rise through the ranks. Therefore, it's important to show the result of all the sales people, not just the select few that are at the top. To improve one's position is something everyone – even the low performer – is interested in.

To reinforce this motivational driver, a manager could comment and encourage sales people who are improving their position even though they haven't taken a top position. Perhaps they have climbed from the bottom to the upper half of the list.

At the same time as it is motivational and gives recognition to the top performers, it also pressures the sales people who are permanently at the bottom of the list. It requires the manager to address this issue in the individual follow-up with these sales people and to initiate special measures when appropriate.

The scoreboard that helped change the attitude

The company sold advanced data communication equipment and there were a lot of people in the sales force that kept a high profile. Not only were they well trained, they had also worked for large international corporations in this industry. During the sales meetings, they usually dominated and promoted ideas on how the company ought to organize and drive the sales. Many ideas were about how other functions should support them, few were about how they could improve themselves.

Harold didn't say so much during the sales meetings, and when he did it was hardly noticed. Perhaps it was his background; perhaps it was his quiet demeanour. This was his first sales position, and previously to that he had been an officer in the military. His résumé didn't contain any prestigious schools or high-profile jobs.

A new chairman started, and he brought with him new routines to the company. Among other things they now started to list and compare how well the sales people were performing. Reports on sales and activities were sent out on a weekly basis and flipcharts were posted in the canteen.

It turned out that Harold sold for considerably more than his colleagues – and made the most customer visits. The attitude towards Harold changed dramatically, and he now got the respect he deserved. In the sales meetings, the colleagues now paid attention to his ideas, which was beneficial for the whole company.

Visualization of activities

In the same way companies visualize results, they can also visualize the key activities the sales people do in order to stimulate the right kind of behavior. Examples of this can be the number of new business opportunities identified, the number of customer visits, number of completed product demonstrations, the number of submitted bids, etc. (We covered activity targets and KPIs in chapter 5.)

Visualization of activities does not differ from how you visualize results. A ranking list with the best performing sales person on top and the rest in descending order is an effective way of visualizing the results. In what format you visualize will be covered a bit later on in this chapter.

Visualized activities also provide a good discussion topic in the one-to-one coaching sessions between sales person and manager to help the sales person will generate enough activities to reach their sales targets. One-to-one coaching will be covered more in-depth in chapter 9.

Recipients and availability

When visualizing, the information should be available to the recipients without them having to look for it. The recipients should at least be the sales group, but in some companies it is open information to the entire company.

For the information to reach its recipients it should be readily available, preferably unavoidable. Solutions that are based on the recipients having to find and compile the information themselves will lead to a lower usage, with less people receiving the information.

Ideally the information should be automatically presented when people log into their systems (intranet, CRM system, etc.) or enter their departments (through billboards – physical or electronic).

Frequency

How often you visualize the performance of the sales people is related to the follow-up frequency and how the targets are designed. If you want to focus on sales performance and have an annual sales target, you could very well use the monthly result when visualizing the performance. This will give a clear month-by-month picture on how the sales people are performing compared to their budgets and compared to each other.

When measuring activities, such as customer visits, it is recommendable to do this on a weekly basis. They are usually formulated as weekly targets, and there is a strong connection to the calendar and planning, which normally is weekly focused.

The key word when talking about frequency is "continuously". You should continuously be able to see the performance of the sales people during the year so it creates a competitive and motivational effect, allowing them the opportunity to improve their ranking. If the results are only presented in arrears, the sales people are faced with fait accompli and there is nothing they can do about their position. Much of the competitive aspect is then gone.

Formats for visualization

The formats of visualization can of course vary, but we have seen some good practices in successful companies worth mentioning.

Sales people's participation

Previously we mentioned that the sales people shouldn't have to find and retrieve the information themselves, since it will lead to less people being exposed to the information. Having said that, a good method to increase the level of commitment from the sales people is if you let them "publish" their success themselves. Examples could be where the sales people write down their orders on a flip chart in the sales department's conference room. When doing this you should beware of presentation techniques relying on advanced technology or props; if the technology is malfunctioning or the props are missing, the solution will not be used. Simplicity is a good guiding principle if you want to ensure the participation from the sales people.

Sales competitions

Running a sales competition means that you set up targets and a set of rules to drive a specific sales initiative during a period of time, where sales people compete against each other and where the winners receive prizes and honour. It capitalizes on the competitive instinct of the sales people. People who have chosen the result-oriented career path of sales tend to be more inclined to compete and having competitions should be a positive element when managing sales organizations.

Sales competitions are, in our experience, very motivating (providing they are executed correctly). It is important that the there is an element of playfulness but even more important that the rules are clear and that the conditions are perceived to be fair. Even if there is a playful tone, it usually becomes quite serious once the competition has started.

Some experience from sales competitions:

- The duration should be short, maximum four months, preferably shorter. This could be dependent on which industry you're in and the typical length of the sales cycle. If the sales cycles are very long, an idea could be to run a "closing competition".
- High frequency of feedback is central for getting a good sales effect.
- Rather have more and inexpensive prizes than a few and expensive ones.
- Run different types of competitions during the year. For example

"Best sales person", "Most sales to new customers", "First order on the new product", etc.

- *Personal* recognition from management on the performance. Having managers, even outside the sales departments, commenting and recognising how the sales people are performing is highly motivational. (Of course, this is a good idea in any circumstance, but the competition format provides a natural opportunity for doing so.)

Gamification

Gamification is a growing trend where you apply game design techniques to motivate people in achieving their goals. The Airlines' Frequent Flyer Programs are usually mentioned as the first example of gamification but sales competitions in their traditional form also contain the same elements.

Gamification takes advantage of people's natural competitiveness to achieve results and status. The concept is based on several components, where the most common ones are called Points, Badges, Levels, Leader boards and Challenges. Over the years we've seen some good examples where these have been applied:

- **Points**. Formulating targets as points can be a way to achieve flexibility in monitoring sales performance. It allows you to convert different measures into points and to present them in a common format. As an example, you may combine both gross margin and order value in the same sales competition.
- **Badges**. Being appointed the sales person of the year, or to the 100%-club, are examples of badges. If this award is displayed at the sales person's work space or as a plaque in the reception area, it becomes a positive announcement of the salesman's success.
- **Levels**. When a company has an established career path, formal recognition of advancement through the levels becomes a motivating factor. You may begin in the tele-sales department, move on to field sales and end up as a key account manager. We have not yet seen that

"Levels" have been applied in the sales competition context, but this could perhaps be a new development.

- **Leader boards.** Ranking lists, comparing all sales people, are frequently used in successful sales organizations, both for monitoring budget performance and for sales competitions.

- **Challenges.** Formulating sales competitions as challenges are common in organizations with a developed sales culture. "The first one to take an order on the new XYZ product will win "a dinner for two" is a simple example.

Sales competition at the IT Company

"We need to do something extra if we want to close the year in a good way." The sales manager was discussing with the CEO. "The delays on the new product has had a demotivating effect on the sales people". The CEO nodded and called the marketing manager and asked him to join them. They also asked the HR manager to sit in on the meeting. After an hour's discussion, they arrived at the following:

The competition ran for two months where the sales people could earn points: Two points were earned for each dollar sold, and one point for each service contract sold. For the newly launched system all points were doubled.

If you reached a certain level already after four weeks you received two crystal champagne glasses and the possibility to earn six glasses in total. When you had earned six glasses you also won a bottle of champagne.

The earned points could be traded for household and leisure goods from a catalogue by the end of the competition. The top three sales people also won a week-end trip to Paris with the sales manager as host.

A ranking list with current status was mailed out twice a week, and daily during the last week of the competition.

The prizes from the catalogue suited the whole family so a catalogue was also sent to the sales people's home address, to create involvement from the families as well.

The competition became a success, both in results and in motivation.

Summary

Visualizing the performance will reinforce the feedback on results and increase motivation. When visualizing performance it can either be on sales results, such as sales versus budget, or on activities, such as number of customer visits or number of new business opportunities. When visualizing performance you want all the sales people to see the performance of the whole sales team. You can also choose to spread the information to other sales teams or even the entire company. To be effective it has to be easy to see the information, preferably unavoidable. The latter means that the recipients of the information will have it presented to them automatically, without them having to ask for it. It could either be on the intranet or posted on billboards in the cafeteria.

It is important that there is a high frequency when visualizing. The formats could also contribute to further strengthen the effect. This could be done through the sales people writing down their results, through the use of sales competitions or through utilizing components of the concept of gamification.

CHAPTER 7

DIMENSION 4:

Forecasting

The perspective of this book is the management of sales organizations, and therefore we will focus on this aspect when dealing with forecasting.

In some companies the forecasting process is an active tool to create a higher effectiveness in the sales organizations. By having the sales people participate in the forecasting process they will get a better understanding of how their results should develop, at the same time as the responsibility for their results is being clarified. Successful elements in a forecasting process for a sales organization are:

- Analysis of how sales to existing customers develops.
- Analysis of business opportunities (i.e. sales pipeline or sales funnel) and by when they close.
- A structured process is in place, where a written forecast is submitted, followed up and discussed between the sales person and responsible manager.
- That the sales people commit to the forecast.

Different forecasting terms

Forecasting is a term that could be used in many contexts.
- General forecasts for how the market or the economy is developing.

- Company specific forecasts related to financial control and budget processes.

- Forecasting as a tool in managing sales organizations.

General forecasts

General forecasts for how the economy is developing in certain areas (employment, prices on certain goods, GNP, etc.) are done by financial and governmental institutions and organizations. The usage of these forecasts varies from company to company. Larger companies use it to a larger extent and some may even have their own resources analysing the data, while smaller companies are less inclined to do so.

Company specific forecasts – forecast vs. budget

Forecasting within companies is closely linked to how the companies work with their budget. When setting a budget (where general forecasts could be used as an input) the company arrives at what results (revenues and costs) the different organizational units are expected to produce for the budget period. Then, when working to reach the budget, companies usually have a forecasting process for estimating how well they are performing to their plan, their budget. Forecasts where they estimate the next month, the next quarter or by the end-of-year are common forecast horizons.

Forecasts of high quality are extremely important: Production planning, procurement of direct material and cash flow, are all examples of areas where good forecasting is critical.

The sales budget

A sales budget is the formal target that a company, a sales department or an individual sales person has for each period. The budget is normally annual, but could be broken down into shorter time spans, such as months or quarters.

The sales forecast

The sales forecast is the instrument by which you analyse and assess how well you perform in relation to your sales budget.

If the budget is set and decided on an annual basis, the forecasts are set at each forecasting occasion – normally each quarter or each month. At these occasions, you assess how well you will perform versus budget for

- next month,

- next quarter, and/or

- by the end of the budget year.

Analyzing customer development

One way to make assessments on future sales is to analyze what the customers have bought so far during the year. If you see a negative deviation in their purchases, compared to previous years or compared to their budgeted volumes, it could be an indication they will buy less from us. This will then influence the outcome for the year, and there is a good reason to lower the sales forecast, unless you can compensate this loss with another customer buying more.

This analysis and forecasting method is well suited where you have customers with continuous, recurring purchases.

Analyzing customer development

The wholesaler of electrical goods had many customers and a fairly small sales force. They had a challenge tracing how their customers were developing in terms of sales. There had been frequent discussions in the past on how to do this better, but other more pressing issues had come in the way.

When the sales manager reviewed the quality control system, which was introduced the previous year, he found a clause that could help them in their efforts. The clause stated that if customers had a negative deviation in sales with more than 25% compared to previous year, they were to be contacted and analyzed. The function was quickly implemented and the sales force got an excellent tool for putting focus on the right customers.

In some of the cases the customers believed they were going to compensate their drop by increasing their purchases later in the year, but sometimes it turned out that the customer had started buying from another wholesaler.

Apart from getting a much better basis for their forecasts, they also got a better understanding for the purchasing needs of their customers and in some cases they were able to win back lost business.

Analysis of business opportunities

Another central element in predicting future sales is to analyze the current business opportunities (i.e. sales pipeline or sales funnel). This method of analysis is well suited when customer purchases come from deals where the sales person plays an instrumental role in driving each deal.

To make a balanced and probable assessment of the revenues you can expect for a specific period, it's important to know when you expect to close the deal (i.e. getting the order), what value the deal will have and how probable it is you will win the deal.

Assessing the probability of winning the deal

To assess the probability that a sales person would win a deal is no simple task. There are two ways of making this assessment: a subjective way and a more objective one

Subjective assessment

A basic form of assessment is to let the sales people estimate the probability of winning the deal based on their knowledge, experience and intuition. This can work well if the manager can verify these assessments by applying his or her own experience when discussing the opportunities with the sales person.

One should be aware of the following pitfalls when using a purely subjective assessment.

- **Some people are more optimistic than others**, which also applies to sales people. It takes an experienced sales manager to factor in each sales person's "level of optimism" when verifying the business opportunities.

- **Tactical considerations from the sales person may disturb the picture**. A sales person may choose to present a low probability for a sales case to avoid questions and attention. "The manager is always on about closing the deals, so I'm laying low until I'm certain I will win it." A sales person who has fallen behind in sales results might, on the other hand, be tempted to make more positive assessments so the work effort won't be questioned. And when the budget targets are being set for the coming year and a large deal is expected during that year, it may be tempting for a sales person to de-emphasize the deal since it is likely to create a more challenging target for next year.

Objective assessment

Professional sales organizations accumulate and use data to calculate the likelihood of a business opportunity moving from one step to the next and eventually becoming an order. This is sometimes referred to as *conversion rate* or *success rate*. For example, you can calculate the percentage of the prospective customers that receive a demonstration of the product, or the percentage of the deals that will be won in the final round. Linked to this you can then standardize the probabilities of winning the deal based on where you are in the sales process. As an example, when customers have received a demonstration of the product, the probability of them buying the product is 60 % (based on experience and statistics from the CRM system).

This method has a clear advantage over the intuitive / subjective method. The tactical element falls away and you get a consistent assessment of all business opportunities. This approach works especially well for larger sales organizations where it is possible to produce statistics from a large number of salespeople and sales projects.

Objective assessment of probabilities

The CEO of the company that sold hardware and software integrated into advanced IT systems had previously worked for several American IT companies. When the responsibility for the Swedish sales organization was assigned to him, he implemented the following standardized probabilities for the sales projects:

20 % The customer has the budget to buy and is talking to us.

40 % We have submitted a proposal and believe that we are on the "short list" – we are one of three potential suppliers.

60 % We are number one on the "short list" – the customers have expressed that they want to buy from us.

80 % We have a "handshake" – we agree on everything, only formal orders (contracts signed) missing.

100 % Orders / contracts signed.

How you handle the probabilities is closely related to how you follow up business opportunities and the different steps in the sales process, which will be covered more thoroughly in chapter 8.

If you believe you will win a deal in a specific month it should influence the forecast for that month. The question is then what forecast value you should use. The full sales value is of course the starting point but considering that you don't win all your deals it is wise to adjust the sales value according to the probability to win it. This *weighted value* is a better representation of the probable outcome and serves as a better value for the forecast, which figure 7.1 illustrates.

Having the sales people report when they plan to close their deals has a positive impact from a sales effectiveness perspective. When they commit to winning a deal a certain month, they will work harder to make that happen. The importance of fulfilling these commitments will be reinforced if the forecasts also are discussed, commented and followed up by their managers.

Customer	Sales Case	Closing Month	Value MEUR	Probability	Weighted value
Company A	New production line	march 2016	240	80 %	192
Company B	4 big machines	march 2016	200	80 %	160
Company C	12 small machines	march 2016	120	60 %	72
Company D	2 big machines	march 2016	100	40 %	40
Company E	18 small machines	march 2016	180	40 %	72
Company F	New production line	march 2016	240	40 %	96
Company G	4 small machines	march 2016	40	20 %	8
Summa			**1,120**		**640**

Figure 7.1 A list of a sales person's business opportunities expected to close a specific month. The values of the opportunities are weighted with the probability to win them, which serves as a better forecasting value.

Forecast Value

In the case example below, you can see how a successful IT company utilizes the strong motivational effect from what in psychology terms is called *commitment and consistency*. People have a desire to be seen as consistent when it comes to words, opinions, attitudes and actions. If we have said that we will win a deal, we are more motivated to make that happen. Cialdini elaborates on this[1], where he mentions Amway Corporation who asks its employees to set individual targets and to commit to them by writing them down on paper.

Weekly commit at the IT Company

For the IT Company *weekly commit* was a central process in driving sales and getting an overview of the current sales cases. Every Monday morning the sales people met their manager for a short meeting where they made a commitment on what cases they were to close during the week.

They discussed the business opportunities, and also talked about the promises that were unfulfilled from the previous week. After meeting their sales teams all the sales managers now met with their sales director. The process from the first meeting was repeated, and now it was the sales managers making their commitments to the sales director. Just as before they also discussed the outcome of the previous week's forecast.

The process kept repeating itself during the day until it had reached the top management, who by the end of the day could overview what the global sales force were committed to sell during the coming week.

Structured process

For the forecasting process to drive sales effectively, the following points need to be addressed:

- **Format.** If you want sales people to commit to their forecast they should be submitted in writing. There are also a couple of practical reasons for that: It needs to be remembered for the next follow-up session, and it should also be easy to pass on the forecast in the organization.

- **Frequency.** How often you should do forecasts is connected to the company's reporting cycle. If you report results for a certain period, it is also natural to provide a forecast how you foresee the coming period. These periods are normally quarterly or monthly, but there are companies (such as in the example above) that have weekly forecasts.

- **Follow-up.** When you submit a forecast, you commit to a future outcome. It is therefore important to follow up how well you fulfil your commitments. Just as you follow up on results vs. budget (which was submitted before the year started) you should follow how performance was compared to the forecast (which was submitted last month). Did the sales people keep their promises?

- **Discussion.** We covered earlier the importance of the sales people getting feedback on their results. This also applies for the sales person's forecast. Is there a gap between the forecasted value and the budgeted value for the rest of the year? Does the sales person need to take any actions to close that gap?

Assuming responsibility for their result

The effect of the points above is that the sales people are made accountable and assume the responsibility for their financial results.

In sales organizations, there is an expectation from top management for the next levels to generate results, which is illustrated by figure 7.2. From the board of directors there is an expectation, a pressure, on the CEO to deliver results. From the CEO there is a pressure on the sales director and from the sales director there is a pressure on the sales manager. Finally, there is a pressure from the sales manager on the sales person.

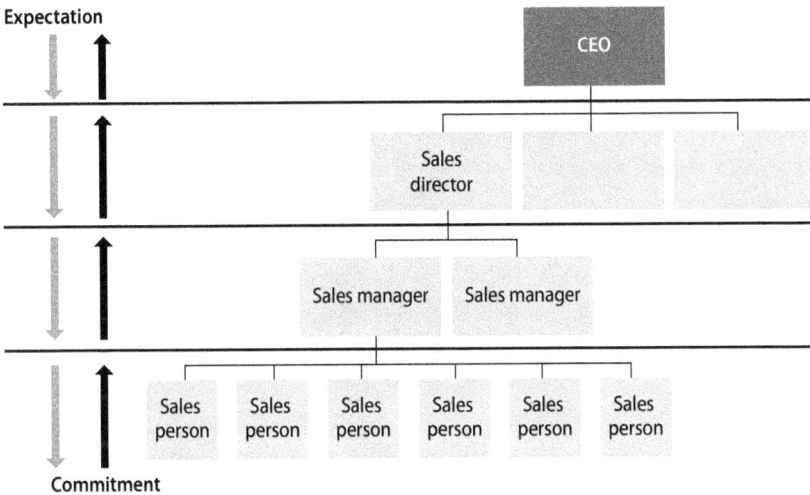

Figure 7.2 The forecasting process as a tool for the company where all levels in the hierarchy commit to their expected results.

Through the forecasting process the company has a tool to make all levels assume the responsibility for their financial results and to live up to their commitments. Since sales people are the ones having the direct contact with the customers, they are the ones who most likely can influence the sales results. It is therefore essential that they participate in the forecasting process.

Summary

Forecasting could be used as a tool to increase the effectiveness in a sales organization. The basis for the forecast is to analyze the development of the customer, for example by looking at purchasing behavior. Another area is the analysis of the business opportunities and when they are expected to close. What is the probability of winning a deal? The probability could be based on an intuitive/subjective assessment or a statistic/objective assessment.

The forecasting process should be defined and used consistently throughout the sales organization. Establishing a forecasting format, reporting frequency, procedures for following up and, finally, providing a forum for discussing the forecast are all appropriate steps. In the end, it will come down to the sales people assuming responsibility and committing themselves to achieve their financial results.

CHAPTER 8

DIMENSION 5:

Opportunity follow-up

Following up on the business opportunities of the sales people is a central task in managing a sales organization. To understand in what stages the sales people are with their opportunities and to support and guide them through the process, the sales management needs

- a clear understanding of the different stages of the sales process
- an overview per sales person of the current opportunities
- a forum for following up each sales person in-person
- documentation of activities and important events associated with each opportunity.

The sales process and its stages

In chapter 2 we covered the sales process, the stages through which an opportunity matures from the first meeting to the final order. The sales manager needs to understand this process in order to follow up, support and guide the sales people with their business opportunities. By having a common definition of the stages that are required to win an order, the sales manager will understand how far a sales person has come in the process. Based on this the manager can better coach the sales person how to take the opportunity to the next stage, and eventually how to win it.

What a sales process looks like for a company is defined by what their customers' buying process looks like. What stages do they need to go through before being able to make a purchase decision and to place the order? A company's sales process therefore becomes a function of their customers' buying process. If it's a complex product they are buying, the customers are likely to go through more stages before they make their decision. The sales process will then have mores stages and take longer time.

Another factor influencing the buying process (and therefore the sales process) is whether the customers use a complex procurement procedure. This is for example the case when bidding for governmental contracts, where law and strict procedures regulate terms of purchasing. A third factor influencing the buying process is whether there are many different roles at the customers involved in the buying process.

To sum it up, it is how the customers buy – not the complexity in what you sell, per se – which dictates what the sales process looks like. The example from the MedTech Company below illustrates this well.

Different sales processes in the MedTech Company

The MedTech Company, which we also told you about in chapter 5, are selling their equipment to hospitals, and not only to doctor's offices. Their sales processes look different depending on what customer segment they are approaching, which figure 8.1 shows.

Doctor's office

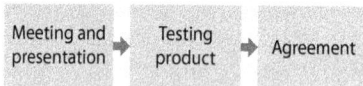

Meeting and presentation ➡ Testing product ➡ Agreement

Hospital

Meeting and qualification ➡ Need analysis ➡ Specificaton ➡ Request for proposal received ➡ Proposal ➡ Agreement

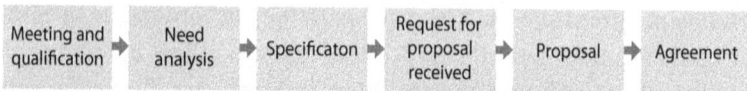

Figure 8.1 The sales processes of the MedTech Company are different for different market segments, even though the products are essentially the same.

At the doctor's office, the doctor is the person deciding about the purchase, and the one the sales people need to meet. At a first meeting the sales people will present the product, pricing, etc. If the doctors are interested they may test the equipment for a month. If they are not happy with the equipment they can return it, but as mentioned in chapter 5, in almost 75 % of the cases they keep it. From the first stage to the last, this process takes six to eight weeks.

When approaching the hospital market the process is much more complex. The first meeting takes place with the laboratory manager at the hospital. If there is an interest, the next step is to find out the needs of the different departments. When the needs have been compiled it will result in a common product specification for the hospital. Since the hospital is governed by public procurement rules, the hospital is required to invite several potential suppliers who could propose a solution matching the product specification. Certainly, the company who has influenced the original product specification is in a better position, since they are more likely to live up to the product requirements.

The MedTech Company write their proposal and send it. Best case, they will win and will sign an agreement with the hospital. This sales process takes much more time – from six months up to a couple of years.

Customer's buying process

What a typical buying process looks like in a business-to-business context has been documented several times.[16] The theory describes eight steps an industrial buyer goes through when facing a purchasing decision:

1. **Need recognition.** A problem is discovered through internal signals (from within the company) or external signals (for example from discussions with external parties, such as sales people or industry colleagues).

2. **Need definition.** A comprehensive description of the problem and how it can be resolved by procuring a certain product.

3. **Product specification.** The buyer specifies what the product should be able to do.

4. **Supplier identification.** Possible suppliers of the product are identified and qualified.

5. **Request for proposal.** Qualified suppliers are invited to propose a solution.

6. **Supplier selection.** Proposals are compared and the best supplier is chosen, with whom an agreement is made.

7. **Specifying order routines**. Methods and routines for ordering, returns, etc. are specified with the chosen supplier.

8. **Supplier evaluation**. The performance of the supplier and the product quality are evaluated after a period. After the evaluation, the buyer may continue, abort or renegotiate the agreement.

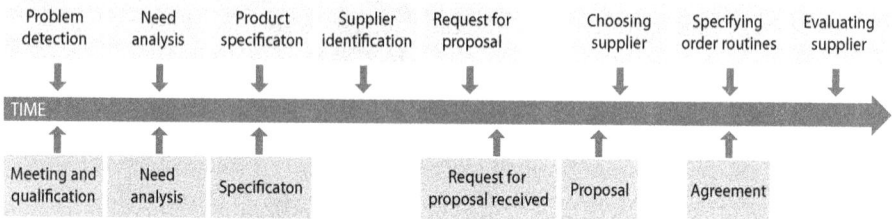

Figure 8.2 The sales process follows the buying process.

Note that this is a generic model. In reality, decision makers and companies are not always as structured and systematic.

Stages in the sales processes

The idea with the different stages in the sales process is to describe the milestones you need to pass to finalize a sales case. Even though *all* customers do not buy in exactly the same way, there is usually a clear, common pattern.

Stages defined as important events

The stages in the sales process should be defined as important events that are *completed*. The stage "proposal", for example, should be defined as the proposal being done and having sent it, not that you are in the process of writing it.

Note, as we mentioned in the beginning of this book, that some companies do not have a sales process worth mentioning. For these organizations, it is not useful with the sales process as a follow-up tool, and neither is trying to contrive such a process. They simply don't work that way. A sales organization approaching retail outlets is an example where a sales process is superfluous. These sales people take their orders directly on their first visit (or try to make the retailer place the order in their systems). They may however have a sales process when they approach the head office of a retail chain, where terms and conditions are agreed upon, before they are allowed to approach the individual retailers. That process, on the other hand, is well worth defining and following up.

See the entire process

In some cases, the sales processes are very short, but it could also be the case that you only see a part of the process. A supplier that believes that the sales process starts when a request for proposal enters the mailbox does not see the entire process and will have a lower chance of winning the deal compared to a supplier who has been part of the process from the very start. That supplier understands the customer and their needs and has created a relation to the customer. An important and, in many cases, deciding factor is whether a supplier has been able to influence the product specification.

Sometimes few but extensive stages

Even if there are few stages in the sales process they can consume a lot of time and effort. Complex products and solutions may require weeks when writing a proposal and providing detailed answers on inquiries. It may also take a long time to make a need analysis when there are many different decision makers, representing different aspects of what is being offered. There could be user aspects, technical aspects and financial aspects, which all need to be addressed to get acceptance for the offered solution.

In complex and time consuming processes like these, following up on the sales people could not be stressed enough to secure a momentum in the sales process. Setting up short-term targets with the sales person could also be a way to break down the stages into smaller steps, e.g. "The technical part of the proposal should be done by Friday".

Selling step by step

The sales process visualises how you sell step-by-step. Apart from using in the internal follow-up, it can also be used to create a good working climate with the customer and to drive the sales cases forward with them:

- The sales process clarifies that the customers need to go through a couple of steps before they can make a purchase decision, which the sales person has to respect and adapt to. Trying to force an early decision will most likely not succeed and might even be perceived as unprofessional by the customer.

- The sales process will help you guide the customer. The customer may be buying what you are offering for the first time and is not sure what the process looks like. By visualizing the process for the customer and suggesting what steps you need to go through, you remove uncertainty and make it easier for the customer to make step-by-step decisions. This will make the entire process move forward at a higher pace.

Opportunity overview

When managing a sales organization, it's vital to have an overview of what business opportunities the sales people are involved in. Firstly, to get a picture of what the future revenue will be (and to be able to forecast, as covered in chapter 7). And secondly to prioritize support and mobilize resources the different sales people are likely to need in driving their opportunities forward.

There are several different tools to create this overview, for example reports from a sales support system (CRM/SFA) or from an excel sheet the sales people update. If there are few sales people, a manual listing on a whiteboard could also be a rudimentary solution. The key is that there is an overview. Figure 8.3 gives an example of what it may look like.

Sales person	Customer	Business opportunity	Closing month	Value EUR ('000)	Proba-bility	Weighted value
E. Carlson	Company A	120 users	Oct 2016	240	80 %	192
E. Carlson	Company B	100 users	Nov 2016	201	80 %	160
E. Carlson	Company C	Corporate license	Jun 2017	249	40 %	100
E. Carlson	Company D	60 users	Oct 2016	121	60 %	73
E. Carlson	Company E	90 users	May 2017	180	40 %	72
E. Carlson	Company F	Corporate license	Mar 2017	120	60 %	72
E. Carlson	Company G	80 users	Nov 2016	156	40 %	63
E. Carlson	Company H	License Upgrade	May 2017	123	40 %	49
E. Carlson	Company I	License Upgrade	Mar 2017	105	40 %	42
E. Carlson	Company J	License Upgrade	Oct 2016	40	60 %	24
E. Carlson	Company K	20 users	Dec 2016	44	40 %	18
E. Carlson	Company L	38 users	Jul 2017	74	20 %	15
E. Carlson	Company M	30 users	Dec 2016	62	20 %	13
E. Carlson	Company N	20 users	Jun 2017	43	20 %	9
E. Carlson	Company O	License Upgrade	Jun 2017	37	20 %	7

Figure 8.3 List of all current business opportunities driven by a sales person. The opportunities are of varying size, have different probabilities of succeeding and are planned to close in different months.

Follow-up

In the follow-up sessions, the sales people present their business opportunities and have the opportunity to discuss them with their sales manager. When going through their business opportunities, vital information about them are presented, such as the size of the opportunity, what stage it's in, when it's estimated to close and how likely it is to win it.

It's recommended to have the follow-up sessions regularly with a pre-defined frequency, and the use of a common language will help in assessing the opportunities.

Discussion and commitment

To just generate a report from a sales automation system is not to be regarded as a follow-up. The central parts of the follow-up are the discussion on how to move the opportunities forward to the next step and the activities the sales person commits to do till the next follow-up session.

Frequency

How often you should report and discuss the business opportunities depends on how long the sales cycle is. If the sales process lasts for a couple of weeks you could have a short follow-up on a weekly basis (as the example earlier, with the MedTech company approaching the doctor's offices). If the sales process lasts for a several months it's recommended to have a monthly follow-up (as the example with the same company approaching hospitals). And, once again, if you don't really have a sales process (as the example of the sales force approaching the retail outlets) there is no point in following up on business opportunities since they appear and close every time the sales person meets the customer. In these cases, rather than following up on business opportunities, you should ensure that the sales people have capacity to meet all their customers in their sales districts so they can close as much business as possible.

Common language

An important aspect of having a pre-defined sales process is that all involved parties have a common language. This allows for clearer communication, better cooperation and fewer misunderstandings. There is also an advantage for the follow-up procedure to have a common language. It gives directly a clear picture on where you are and what needs to be done with the different business opportunities. Being in the proposal stage or in the need analysis stage requires no further explanation, as you know directly how far you've come in the process. The discussion could then be focused on what needs to be done in order to move the opportunity forward.

Documenting important events and activities

Just as the business opportunities are registered in some sort of system, it's also important to log important events, activities and documents that are associated with the business opportunity and the customer. It's a question of protecting the investment the company has done to generate the opportunity. Otherwise, what happens if the sales person leaves the company? If the company has no logging of the business opportunity and important events connected to it, the opportunity will be lost. If the sales person has left the company to join a competitor, that sales person may now approach the customer with a competitive offer. Then you have invested in developing an opportunity that the competition will harvest.

If a sales person leaves the company, you must be able to continue working with that person's opportunities. Apart from knowing who they are, you also need access to important documents and agreements connected to that opportunity.

Summary

To follow up on the business opportunities of the sales people is a central task when managing a sales organization. The sales process is a series of events leading up to a sale, and it's a reflection of the customer's buying process. The stages in the sales process visualizes how a sales person drives an opportunity forward, which is used in the internal follow-up.

The sales manager needs to have an overview of all business opportunities of the sales organization. Therefore, these need to be logged and stored in an easily retrievable way, such as in a CRM system.

To have sales people present and discuss their opportunities with their manager is the foundation for a good following-up process, which should lead to moving the opportunities forward. How often you should follow up is dependent on the length of the sales process.

To report and log important events and documents connected to the opportunity is a way for the company to protect the investment they have made in the customer relationship.

CHAPTER 9

DIMENSION 6:

Individual coaching & follow-up

In earlier chapters, we have covered the follow-ups sales managers do with their sales people when going through results, forecasts and business opportunities. In the next chapter, we will cover the follow-up of the sales peoples' activities. In this chapter, we are focusing on the importance of at least one of these follow-ups being on an individual basis. To maximize the impact of this session, it is important that, in addition to being individual, it is also conducted frequently and according to a pre-defined pattern.

Why individual follow-up

The reason for having an individual follow-up session could be summarized in three points.

- The sales person is recognized and has the manager's undivided attention.
- To coach the sales person effectively.
- Opportunity to bring up sensitive or difficult issues.

To be acknowledged

There is a strong motivational force in a manager recognizing the individual employee. This is also true for sales people. The fact that they have chosen an independent profession, which sales often is, does not change this.

The large Tech Company

"You deliver good results, but your 700 employees have a lower job sat-isfaction than the rest of the company," the CEO glared at business unit manager who gritted his teeth.

The management team had just gone through the annual employee satisfaction survey, and the business unit manager had just received the worst result of them all. At the same time, his business unit delivered good results so why wasn't everyone happy?

The low scores in the survey were surprising and he didn't quite know how to resolve them. The CEO gave no concrete advice and his colleagues in the management team had just shrugged.

He decided to bring it up with the external consultant that was coach-ing him regularly. The consultant advised him to have short individual sessions weekly with his direct reports to follow up on how the week had been and what the plans were for next week. These, in turn, would do the same to their direct reports and so forth until all employees in the busi-ness unit had met their manager for 15-20 minutes each week.

About a year later, when the consultant came for one of his coaching sessions, he met a beaming business unit manager. They had just con-ducted a new employee satisfaction survey; not only had the business unit manager improved his results, but he was now topping the charts with the highest percentage of satisfied employees in the company.

The only real change was the introduction of the weekly meetings throughout the business unit.

Coaching

The individual meeting allows for intimacy and openness, where the man-ager can give candid feedback on the sales person's performance. It is a good environment for coaching and, when necessary, for corrective measures.

There will always be large differences between different sales people, their personalities and experiences, and therefore their need for coaching. A new sales person may need support and guidance in how to book a meeting over the phone, and an experienced sales person may need to improve negotiation skills. It is more effective and efficient to coach *individually*, where the discussion can be tailored to the need of the individual sales person.

The sales manager will also get good input to the coaching when joining a sales person in the field, visiting customers. After all, interacting with the customer is when the sales people do their real work. It's a dimension of its own in our model and will therefore be covered in more detail in chapter 11.

Addressing sensitive issues

The individual meeting will allow you to bring up sensitive issues and criticism, which would be inappropriate to address in a team meeting.

An example of a sensitive issue could be the personal situation of the sales person. Relations to colleagues, family problems, and health problems are types of issues that influence the performance of the sales person. The individual meeting will provide a forum where these issues may be addressed early and handled with integrity.

Follow-up frequency

How often should a manager have an individual follow-up with the sales people? It's a good idea to adapt to the follow-up sessions that are most likely already in place, for example when you follow-up on key activities or financial results.

The follow-up on *key activities*, for example customer visits or other KPIs, are closely connected to the calendar of the sales person: "What happened this week – what is planned for next week?" is a normal routine for follow-up and is natural to do on a weekly basis.

How often you follow-up on *results*, which we also described in chapter 5, is connected to how the targets are formulated. If you have annual targets (which is very common in sales forces) it is appropriate to do monthly follow-ups. If the targets are monthly, weekly follow-ups are recommendable.

Pre-defined pattern

As we mentioned in the introduction of this chapter, it is important that the follow-up sessions follow a pre-defined pattern.

Agenda

The meeting should have a specific purpose where you follow up and discuss central topics related to the sales people reaching their targets. This could either be results or key activities, necessary to generate the results. If you don't have a specific purpose with the meeting, neither manager nor sales person will come prepared to it and there is a risk you will never address important – and sometimes sensitive – subjects.

If the same topics are always discussed, it makes preparations easier for both the manager and the sales person. This leads to productive meetings.

A basic agenda for weekly one-to-one meetings could look like this:

- What activities did you do last week?
- What was the result?
- What activities are planned for next week?
- What targets do we set for next week?

A basic agenda for monthly one-to-one meetings could contain the following topics:

- What is your result year-to-date compared to budget?
- What are your current business opportunities?
- Which business opportunities are new? Which ones are lost?
- What is your forecast for next month and end-of-year?
- How many (and which) of your customers have you visited during the month?

Reserved time

For the meeting to take place it needs to be booked or scheduled.

Sometimes you will encounter sales managers that believe they can address these topics "whenever", since they see and talk to the sales people daily and believe they have an open atmosphere.

The problem with this informal approach is that, even though they have daily contact with the sales people, they don't systematically discuss the important topics. The sales person will thereby miss out on necessary coaching and the company will lose productivity.

How much time for the follow-up session?

How much time you should allocate depends on several factors. Based on our experience, 20 minutes should suffice for a weekly one-on-one with an agenda similar to the one outlined above. For a monthly session, covering the topics above, you would more likely need 60 minutes.

Consistency

By consistency we mean that you should follow-up and coach all sales people.

The perception should not be that you only follow-up and coach low performing sales people. The individual meeting will then be perceived as a punishment. You want all your sales people to be acknowledged, feel motivated and perform even better.

Unfortunately, a lot of sales managers spend a disproportional amount of time on "problem sales people", which usually is a small portion of the sales force and in some cases are beyond salvage. The opposite situation could also be true, where successful sales people make sure to get the attention and support from the sales manager.

To get a strong impact in sales performance it is important to lift the majority of the sales people (which are grouped in the middle) so they perform like high performing sales people. This will have a much higher impact than spending the time on trying to lift a group of low performing sales people, who are usually difficult to develop.

Coaching theory

If a sales manager gives praise to a sales person for a specific behavior the likelihood increases for the sales person to repeat that behavior. This simple logic goes back to the American psychologist B.F. Skinner's[17] research in the 1930's. Sales coaching can be defined as "a series of dialogues and activities where feedback and encouragement is given to a sales person in order to increase the performance of that sales person".[18]

Research about the difference in coaching focuses of "output feedback" (i.e. achieved results) and "behavioral feedback" (behaviors of the sales person) has shown the following:

- Feedback on a sales person's positive results seems to be the most effective way to increase the performance.

- Positive feedback focusing on the sales person's behavior has a stronger positive effect on job satisfaction.

- Negative feedback has a lower motivational effect than positive feedback, irrespective if it's on result or on behavior. Interestingly enough, feedback on negative results does not seem to diminish how happy the sales person is with the sales manager, which means that a sales manager could react on weak performances without the sales person becoming miserable.[19]

Summary

Individual follow-up and coaching of sales people are important. Of all the regular meetings the sales manager has with sales people, at least one should be on individual basis; the sales person is acknowledged, the coaching becomes more effective and there is an opportunity to bring up sensitive topics.

Individual follow-up could either be on results or key activities, e.g. customer visits. Key activities lead to results: The more business opportunities you drive, the more orders you are likely to generate, as an example. Monitoring key activities is therefore an important aspect when following up and coaching.

The individual meetings should have a pre-defined purpose and an agenda. The meetings should also be booked or scheduled and be performed consistently throughout the sales force.

CHAPTER 10

DIMENSION 7:

Activity levels and planning

Successful companies ensure that they have high activity levels and a high level of quality in their customer contacts.

- They measure and target the number of customer contacts the sales people should have.
- There is a support structure in place to ensure a high activity level.
- The number of customer contacts is sufficient to reach the sales targets.
- The contacts are made with those customers who are potentially profitable to the company.

Measuring and targeting the number of customer contacts

In a field sales organization, the customer visit is a central activity.

The direct customer contacts are required to drive the sales process from the first meeting to successfully closing the order. You may, for example, meet the customer when creating an interest for your offering, when demonstrating the solution, and finally when going through your proposal with the customer. The more customer meetings a sales organization can produce, the more sales opportunities they are capable of driving.

Apart from driving specific sales opportunities, the sales people meet the customers for other reasons. These meetings could be status and follow-up meetings, which come natural in a customer-supplier relationship. But they could also be social visits to maintain the customer relationship and meetings aimed at discovering new sales opportunities. The more customer meetings a sales organization is able to produce, the more customers they are capable of covering during a year.

The number of customer meetings determines how many sales opportunities and how many customers an organization is capable of handling. The customer meeting is therefore a good performance measure (or KPI, which we covered in chapter 5) for a field sales organization.

When targeting and measuring customer meetings, it's important not to forget the quality aspect of these meetings. Just measuring the number of meetings is not enough – you also need to follow-up (as covered below) the sales people to ensure the quality aspect. One way of assessing the quality is to see whether they meet the right type of customer and decision maker, and that the purpose of the meeting is to drive business.

Support structure to ensure high activity levels

To get high activity levels – where the sales people do a lot of customer meetings – does not happen by just measuring and targeting the number of sales meeting. It requires the organization to set up a structure supporting the sales people to achieve high activity levels.

Individual coaching

As we covered earlier, in chapter 6, the individual coaching session is an excellent forum to follow up customer meetings. The weekly session where the customer meetings is the main subject will increase the number of customer meetings as well as safeguard the quality by ensuring that the sales people do the right type of visits.

Support in planning

To be able to produce as many customer meetings as possible in the available time, scheduling of some activities could be helpful:

- **Scheduling of booking time.** An obstacle for achieving a high activity level is that it's time consuming to book the meetings in the first place. It takes a substantial amount of time to e-mail and phone customers to book meetings with them, and sales people tend to underestimate the effort needed. A good way to resolve this is for the company to schedule booking time for their sales people, as in the example below. We have noted that in industries where the need to book customer meetings is low or non-existent (for example sales forces approaching retail outlets), the activity levels are considerably higher than in industries where you are required to book in advance. Furthermore, in companies using a combination of "drop-in" visits and meetings booked in advance, the sales people doing the drop-in visits produce more than twice as many visits, even though they sell the same product.

Book meetings

The vending machine company had what they called customer dating sessions every Monday morning. John had laughed the first time he heard about this as a new sales person. But he felt it was a good working practice, and it helped him make those calls that sometimes were tough to make.

The customer dating sessions were mandatory for everyone in the sales force where all the sales teams throughout the country called customers in their respective territory with the sole purpose to book meetings for the coming weeks. The goal was to book as many meetings as possible during the two hours it lasted.

After half the time, all the groups took a short break where the sales people reported how many calls they had made and how many meetings they had been able to book.

They reported either in the meeting room, or if they were located in a field office, they called in via phone. The same procedure was repeated when the session ended, and at that time the company gave a symbolic prize to the winner in each group. John noticed that he was not alone in his desire to win.

- **Scheduling customer time and internal time.** This means that you reserve time in the calendar for all the types of activities a sales person needs to do. By doing this you also clarify the expectation that the sales people should do many customer meetings and limit internal and less productive tasks. An example of this could be seen in figure 10.1 below. Sales people using these models achieve substantial productivity gains even if they don't always succeed in keeping all the allocated slots for their original purposes.

	Monday	Tuesday	Wednesday	Thursday	Friday
08:00					Telephone time - book meetings
09:00	Internal meetings and admin	Customer meeting 1	Customer meeting 5	Customer meeting 9	
10:00					Reporting into CRM
11:00	Sales team meeting	Customer meeting 2	Customer meeting 6	Customer meeting 10	
12:00	LUNCH				
13:00	Prepera-tions for the weekly customer meetings	Customer meeting 3	Customer meeting 7	Customer meeting 11	Weekly 1-2-1
14:00					Actions and proposals form the week
15:00		Customer meeting 4	Customer meeting 8	Customer meeting 12	
16:00					

Figure 10.1 An example from a well-planned sales person's calendar.

Prioritized customer base

A basic method for focusing on the quality aspect when doing customer meetings is to prioritize the customer base, as we covered in chapter 4. This helps the sales person to target the right type of customer and the right decision maker, and also helps the sales manager in his follow-up.

Sufficient number of customer meetings

How do you calculate the number of customer meetings the company needs to do to achieve their targets? To answer that question you need to break down the financial targets and translate them to customer meetings. In reaching the targets you need to win a certain amount of deals and/or you need to cover a certain number of customers. To estimate this is just straightforward math.

Number of deals necessary to reach the target

By calculating the average deal size, you can quickly see how many deals you need to win in order to reach your annual revenue target. After that you can calculate how many customer meetings you need to do to win all these deals. What you need to consider is the following:

- How many times on average do you need to meet a customer before winning a deal?
- Of all the sales opportunities you participate in, how many of those deals do you win in the end?
- Of all the business opportunities you lose, when in the sales process do you lose them in general?

Let's review the example in figure 10.2. There we can see that the company needs to win 200 deals with an average deal size of 50,000 EUR to reach their annual sales budget. Since the company, based on experience, wins 25 % of the sales opportunities they participate in, they need to drive 800 sales opportunities. In the 200 cases they win the deal, they meet the customer four times on average. In the 600 cases where they lose, they do on average two meetings with the customer before the customer decides to go with another supplier. In total the company needs to do 2,000 meetings in order to reach the annual budget.

$$\frac{10{,}000 \text{ KEUR in annual target}}{50 \text{ KEUR} / \text{ average deal}} \quad = \quad 200 \text{ deals}$$

$$\frac{200 \text{ deals}}{25\% \text{ success factor}} \quad = \quad 800 \text{ opportunites}$$

$$200 \text{ won deals} \times 4 \text{ visits} \quad = \quad 800 \text{ visits}$$

$$600 \text{ lost deals} \times 2 \text{ visits} \quad = \quad 1{,}200 \text{ visits}$$

$$\text{Visits required during the year} \quad = \quad 2{,}000 \text{ visits}$$

Figure 10.2 Calculating the number of deals and meetings needed in order to reach the targets.

Number of customers that needs to be covered to reach the target

In calculating this, the link between revenue targets and number of meetings needed is not as strong as when calculating meetings and deals as shown in figure 10.2 above. This approach is more applicable when sales does not come from deals the sales people are driving, but rather from repetitive purchases from the customers (perhaps without the sales people being involved in the procurement). An example of this is sales forces that approach retail outlets.

The method for calculating the number of meetings needed is more based on the assumption that a certain activity level is needed to stimulate demand for the company's products and to ensure loyalty and the future purchase volume.

In order to reach the annual sales budget the company wants to ensure that the customers are met on a regular basis. The target for how often to meet the customers could vary between customer types. Prioritized customers, with the potential for high purchase volumes, are usually visited with a higher frequency.

The more visits a sales organization is able to produce, the more customers they will be able to cover. In figure 10.3 below, the hypothetical company has 1 000 customers. To ensure the customers' purchase volumes, the company wants the sales people to visit the 200 largest customers six times a year, the medium sized customers three times a year, and the smallest customers once a year. In total this means that the sales organization needs to produce 2 800 visits.

Total number of customers		1,000
200 major customers visited 6 times / year	=	1,200 visits
400 midsize customers visited 3 times / year	=	1,200 visits
400 small customers visited 1 time / year	=	400 visits
Visits required during the year	=	2,800 visits

Figure 10.3 Calculating the number of customers and meetings needed in order to reach the targets.

Profitable customer contacts

Another way to approach the topic of customer meetings is by looking at the *cost* of the customer meeting. You do an analysis of all the activities required to do a customer meeting and allocate the expenses for these activities. In this way you can obtain an approximate cost for a customer meeting. However, note that you need to regard a series of customer meetings and activities in order to do a more exact analysis.

This methodology could also be used for analyzing other parts of the company, and a term which is frequently used is *activity based costing* (ABC calculation).

Activity Based Costing

To identify and allocate costs to activities, and to compare them with what these costs and activities resulted in, became a popular accounting practice during the 1980's and 90's. During this period Kaplan and Bruns defined Activity Based Costing (ABC)[20].

The steps in implementing ABC could be described in the following, simplified way:

1. Identify activities by analysing the processes needed to achieve a certain output.

2. Allocate costs to the activities, direct and indirect.

3. Identify the outputs of the processes and activities.

4. Allocate activity costs to the output.

How big the deal must be

By calculating the costs for a customer meeting, you can also calculate the cost of doing business since winning a deal requires a series of meetings. This cost should be compared with the expected gross profit for the deal. If the cost for the customer meetings is expected to surpass the expected gross profit, the deal is not profitable to pursue with a sales person. (However, it may still be of interest to approach the customer through other channels, such as tele-sales.)

In the example in figure 10.4, the deal is profitable. It costs 5,000 EUR to win a deal (all costs included) and the company's gross profit is 15,000 EUR. The profit from the deal is therefore 10,000 EUR. If the sales margin had been only 10% and the company had only received 5,000 EUR in gross profit, the deal would not have been profitable at all.

An analysis like this will help you decide what size the deals need to be in order to justify being approached by a field sales force.

However, note that these figures are not static. The more customer meetings a sales organization can produce, without recruiting more sales people, the lower the cost per sales meeting. Therefore, the cost of winning a deal

Annual cost for the sales team : 1,000 KEUR
• Salaries, bonuses, pension, etc
• Cars and travel expenses
• Representation
• IT, office supplies and miscellaneous

No. of customer visits by the team :
2,000 visits

Cost per visit (1,000 KEUR / 2,000) :   **Revenue per deal** :
500 EUR   50,000 EUR

No. of visits to win an average deal   **Sales Margin:**
Incl. visits on lost deals: 30%
10

Cost per deal :   **Gross profit per deal** :
5,000 EUR   15,000 EUR

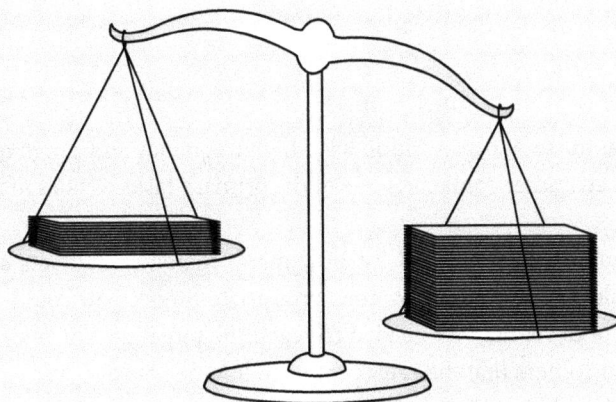

Figure 10.4 Example on how to calculate the profitability in a deal.

will be lower. Simultaneously, the cost of doing business will also go down if the company has a higher success factor. Then they will win a higher proportion of deals and not spend as much time on sales opportunities that they lose in the end.

How much a customer must buy for

Another way to assess the profitability of the customer meetings is to review how much a customer has potential to buy during a certain period. The gross profit of this revenue needs to be compared to how much it costs to do business with the customer.

If we assume, in line with the example in figure 10.4, that a sales meeting costs 500 EUR and that we meet the customer six times a year, the customer must yield more than 3,000 EUR in gross profit a year to be profitable. Otherwise it's not profitable to have such a high meeting frequency with this customer. This analysis will tell you the purchase volumes a customer must have in order to justify a certain number of customer meetings.

To assess the profitability of a specific customer, you need to calculate net margin of that customer.[21] From the gross margin you also deduct the sales cost and other potential direct costs (such as costs for administration, product development and storage) that are associated with that specific customer.

Summary

Ensuring that the sales organization has a high frequency and a high quality level in their customer contacts is one of the primary tasks of sales management.

Targets should be established for how many customer contacts a sales person should have. In deciding the appropriate target, you could assess the number of deals that are needed to reach the target and/or review the number of customers that the sales person should be able to cover.

To actually achieve a high activity level, it's vital to coach and follow-up sales people. An individual weekly meeting, where you review the activities of the past and coming week is a good routine. Other measures to achieve this include helping the sales people to structure their work by scheduling key activities, such as booking of customer meetings and allocating customer time. Another key component is the quality aspect, and how you help the sales people to prioritize so they meet the right customers and the right decision makers.

To ensure that the customer meetings are profitable you can calculate their cost and compare it with the gross profit you expect from a potential deal. You can also assess the customers' potential purchase volume. The gross profit from this volume should then be weighed against the sales cost for the customer, where the meeting cost is an integral part.

CHAPTER 11

DIMENSION 8:

Joint field visits

Developing the sales people and ensuring that they possess the right qualities are important responsibilities for the sales management. It's recommendable to do this when the sales people perform their primary task – interacting with customers. Joint customer visits are therefore a natural task for sales management. Important parts of this dimension are:

- There should be a clear purpose with the visits.
- The experiences from these visits should be a basis for feedback and coaching of the sales people.
- Working with a combination of announced and unannounced joint visits.

Purpose: Developing and ensuring quality of sales people

It's quite common for sales managers to join their sales people in meeting customers. The sales situations could dictate that the managers come along in order to bring decision power to the meeting (at a negotiation for example) or that they come along to show respect for the customer. Joint meetings could also be driven by the managers' wish to form his/her own opinion of the customers and not only rely on the picture conveyed by the sales people.

What this dimension of our model focuses on, however, is the joint customer meeting with the purpose of understanding and ensuring the quality of the sales person and how this person can develop further. This requires the manager to not take over the meeting, to allow the sales person to freely and naturally interact with the customer.

What the manager observes during the customer meeting will be the basis for future feedback and coaching of the sales person, where good and desirable behavior is reinforced and undesirable behavior is corrected. Focusing on one or a few points is recommendable: One positive aspect and one area to improve from the sales visit. Positive feedback will have a better effect and lead to a higher job satisfaction than negative feedback. Insights on how one's behavior is perceived are a good basis for change. To lead the sales person to this insight through open questions – for example, "What do you feel went well and not so well?" – and questions on consequences – "What do you think happens if you accept a price reduction?" – is a proven method when developing people.

This quality assurance and coaching is of extra importance for newly recruited sales people, but even experienced sales people should be coached.

Frequency

A good rule of thumb is that all sales people should be out on a joint visit together with his or her manager once a month. For a new sales person the frequency could be higher, while a seasoned sales person probably requires lower frequency.

In our experience, managers often have a positive attitude towards visiting customers with the sales people, but they don't do it to the extent that is desired. In addition, it is very rare that the expressed purpose is to listen and observe their sales people.

The companies that succeed-in making this happen have clear expectations of how often the sales managers should join their sales people in the field. In some companies the sales management will even reserve some days every month, for this purpose.

Joint visits at the large document management company

The new sales director was recruited from outside the company and the expectations were high. The new corporate concepts on how to professionalize the sales organization and increase sales were to be implemented.

One of the components was that team leaders and regional managers were expected to join the sales people out in the field, visiting customers. The target was that they should spend at least one day a week in the field with one of the 130 sales people. The sales director decided that she also should be part of this initiative, even though she would not be able to commit a full day a week. She had also read about the benefits of doing the joint visits unannounced, and she was eager to try it. With a slight sense of trepidation, she decided her approach:

She turned up at the regional office and told the regional manager that she wanted to accompany a sales person during the day. She declined the regional manager's proposal of finding a suitable candidate, and instead looked up one of the team leaders at random. Together they selected a sales person on his way out in the field.

She told the sales person she wanted to come along for all the visits during the day, that she would only sit in on the meetings and listen, and that the sales person should just introduce her as a colleague. "This is NN and she is travelling with me today".

After each visit the sales director commented on *one* positive point and if needed *one* negative point, never more than that.

"It was really good that you were able to agree and book the next step with the customer! But hey, don't forget to introduce yourself properly in the reception. It's not just a matter of courtesy, the person sitting there could be the one helping you get hold of the right person."

The first day was a positive experience for both the sales director and the sales person. Unannounced visits were introduced as a new routine, and the sales director's good example increased the motivation among team leaders and regional managers.

Summary

Sales people do their primary work in direct contact with their customers. To join the sales people in their customer meetings is an important part of understanding the quality of how they perform professionally and how they can develop further, which should be the focus of the joint meeting. The responsible manager should accompany each sales person once a month as a good rule of thumb.

The manager's observations from the joint sales calls should be used for feedback and coaching of the sales person. You reinforce desired behavior and correct undesired ones. Commenting a few points is enough, with typically one good point to reinforce and one point to improve.

CHAPTER 12

DIMENSION 9:

Performance improvement program

How to handle sales people who are not performing is an issue for virtually all sales organizations. A humane, efficient and in some countries, legally required way (from a labor law perspective) to approach the issue is to establish a formal action plan for performance improvement. When doing so, the following aspects are important:

- Deciding when the action plan should be initiated. A pre-requisite for this is that the lowest acceptable performance level is defined.
- That the guidelines are clear and that the content of the action plan is communicated to the sales organization.
- The action plan is initiated consistently when the defined performance level is reached.

Initiating the action plan

When a sales person falls behind in performance, the action plan should be initiated in a constructive and pre-defined way. The purpose of the plan is to investigate why the performance is low and to decide what actions are needed to improve the performance.

There are two basic scenarios when dealing with low performance in sales organizations:

- When the performance of a sales person drops below the lowest acceptable performance level.

- When a newly recruited sales person does not reach up to an acceptable performance level.

In both these cases the company should define what the lowest acceptable performance level is. In the first case, it could be expressed as the sales person's performance versus budget. In the second case, it could be expressed as the sales person's performance in relation to calendar time.

Clear performance levels

"It's important that everyone in the sales force understands why a certain individual is subject to extra attention and a more frequent follow-up", said the sales director to the newly recruited team leader. "If they don't understand why these actions are taken, a feeling of insecurity is likely to spread, which could be demotivating. They might envision a choleric boss waving his gun. Who's the next to shoot?" The sales director laughed when he said it, but he spoke from a long experience.

"In our company we always initiate an action plan when a sales person, after a quarter, falls behind with 30 % or more compared to budget. Simultaneously, an action plan will be initiated when a new sales rep has not sold for more than 100,000 EUR in six months. We make sure everyone knows this. It's even in the employee handbook."

Clear guidelines and communication

A formal action plan for performance improvement should have clear guidelines for when to initiate and how to handle the situation when the performance level is unsatisfactory. In our work with different sales organizations, we have noticed that where there is no plan for how to handle low performance, there is generally a frustration shared among mid- and high performers that the company seems to be ignoring this.

We have also noticed that newly recruited sales people appreciate clear expectations on how much ramp-up time they have before they are expected to perform normally. If the company has a complex offering this could take time. To clarify this ramp-up time will give the new sales people peace of mind, where they don't need to worry about how their performance is perceived.

The content of the action plan and a description of the process could very well be included in the employee handbook. It is, after all, something that regulates the employer-employee relationship.

Content of the action plan

1. **Investigation.** First you need to find the reasons for the low performance. Are there personal things that are interfering? Is the activity level sufficient? Does the sales person have a fair sales territory compared to the other sales people?

2. **Formulating targets.** What do we want the sales person to achieve in the short term to show that a change has occurred? What financial results should be achieved and/or what activities should be concluded within a certain time span?

3. **Follow-up.** Follow-up should be done as soon as possible and with a high frequency. If activities are to be completed they should be followed up on a weekly basis. Financial results need to be followed up at least monthly. It's important to decide how long the follow-up period should be before you establish whether the sales person has improved, or whether other measures need to be taken. In the end, it's a question of whether the sales person is suitable for the sales role or not.

4. **Documentation.** To properly document the action plan and the follow-up sessions serves multiple purposes. It shows how the sales person follows the agreed plan and how the results develop. It also helps the discussions from a labor law perspective, should the sales person need to be removed from the sales role.

Consistent implementation

It is vital that you are consistent in the implementation of the action plan, and that there is no special treatment. There is an objectivity aspect in having a performance improvement program that is initiated irrespective of all other circumstances. The reason for sitting down and discussing this with a sales person is strictly a matter of performance, not whether that person is popular with the manager or not. If you follow this simple rule there is no drama or unnecessary speculation once you have to deal with a situation like this.

Summary

A humane and effective way of handling low performing sales people is to establish an action plan for performance improvement. This plan should be initiated without exceptions when a sales person falls under a pre-defined performance level, or when a newly recruited sales person has problems reaching a certain level within a specified time frame.

The individual action plan is produced by the manager, with the help and input from the sales person in question. It starts with investigating the possible reasons for low performance, followed by setting targets for what the sales person should achieve in the short run, both in activities and in results. Follow-up sessions are then planned and conducted with high frequency. Finally, every part of the process is documented in written form.

To implement the program consistently, where no special treatment occurs and where everybody who falls behind is subject to the action plan, is important to gain acceptance and trust in the organization.

PART III

Making it happen

CHAPTER 13

Implementing the nine dimensions

In the second part of the book we have described nine performance areas or dimensions, and you have surely noticed that there is interdependence between many of them. To make an assessment of what the proper activity levels are (chapter 10), you need to know the customer structure (chapter 4) and what effort is needed in driving the deals (chapter 8). To establish the lowest acceptable performance level versus budget (chapter 12) you need to know sales people's budget (chapter 5). Simultaneously, you need to know the budgets if you want to visualize how sales people perform versus budget on a scoreboard (chapter 6).

In this chapter we will cover the order in which you should implement the nine dimensions, and we describe a meeting structure helping the sales organization in achieving and maintaining the desirable changes.

Implementing the model

The basis for a successful implementation of the nine dimensions is to first establish the basic structure, then set the procedures for day-to-day management, and finally to set up the measures for quality assurance:

- **Establish the basic structure first.** The first two dimensions (chapter 4 and 5) describe how you structure your sales territories and how you set targets for the sales people. It's the foundation when managing a sales organization, and also sets the framework for the other dimensions. In these two dimensions you also find basic follow-up procedures.

- **Establish the on-going management processes.** The following five dimensions (chapters 6–10) cover the day-to-day management processes where you visualize results, where sales people commit to their forecasts, where you follow-up on business opportunities, how you coach and follow-up sales people individually, and how you ensure that the sales people have a sufficient activity level.
- **Finalize with quality assurance.** The last two dimensions (Chapter 11 and 12) cover the tools available for management to assure the quality of the sales people's work and the procedure for correcting when the performance is low.

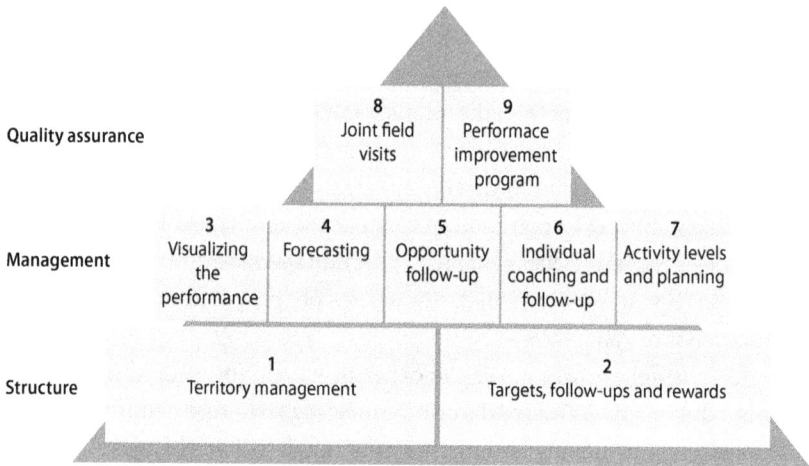

Figure 13.1 Relationship between the nine dimensions

When organizing sales for the first time

A company that has just established a sales organization needs to start setting up basic working practices on which they can develop further:

- Deciding which customers to approach – and by which sales person.
- Set targets for what the sales people should achieve – both in financial terms and other KPIs (for example, how many customers they are expected to cover during a year).
- Follow up on how their business opportunities develop.

When these elements are in place, the company can refine their processes and develop their skills further to encompass all nine dimensions.

Example from a start-up company

The newly founded company had developed an energy bar specially designed for young sports people. An independent manufacturer produced the bar based on the company's recipe, which specifically satisfied the nutrition needs of youths and catered for an optimal recovery after sports activities. The owners of the company had been out meeting several sports clubs and had quickly sold out their first batch of bars. They decided to place a new, much bigger order giving them a considerable cost benefit.

Now they really needed to succeed in their sales effort, and they had to approach a wider part of the market with more resources and in a more structured way than before. Firstly, they decided to continue their direct sales approach to sports clubs. These should then sell the products to the sporting youths (and their parents) which would be a welcome contribution to the club's finances.

Since the company now needed to expand in a larger part of the country, they selected the cities where they wanted to focus, and listed all the sports clubs. After that they recruited students from the local universities that could work as sales people parallel to their studies. The company assigned each sales person with a list of interesting sports clubs that they were to approach in their sales district.

The company set a target for how much they expected the sales people to sell for, and since the salary was based wholly on commission, they also presented a calculated target salary which was very attractive if they reached their targets.

On top of the revenue target, there was also a target for which sports clubs to visit first, and how many clubs to visit every week. If the sales person didn't get started in approaching the sports club, the company wanted to have the possibility to transfer the customer to another sales person.

To ensure that the sales people got started they had a telephone meeting every week where they followed up on sales figures and which customers that had been contacted during the week.

Example from an established commercial bank

"We have no sales culture in the bank", said the marketing manager. "At least not when it comes to advanced financing solutions. What if our people were as sharp as our corporate finance, when it comes to working proactively?"

"But we do", said the department manager. "It's just that the sales responsibility lies with the branch offices."

They were discussing this during a coffee break at the head office. The central business unit of the bank was helping the branch offices in creating advanced financing solutions for the corporate customers.

The business unit was called upon when the branch offices themselves were unable to solve the financing needs of their customers. However, the management for the business unit, which also had a profit and loss responsibility, believed they could generate higher revenues for themselves and for the branch offices – if they were more proactive in their customer approach.

They decided to become more sales oriented and set up a framework for how to achieve this.

First, they prioritized all their customers and allocated the more important ones to the employees who were to assume the sales responsibilities (in some cases this was on top of normal tasks). The branch offices were also allocated, because the employees needed to coordinate the customer contacts. This meant that there was one sales responsible person for each important customer and each branch office. Now the approach plan was in place.

"You get what you measure ... We need clear and measurable targets", said the marketing manager.

A couple of targets were set.

- To start with they set an annual target for the business volume they wanted to achieve, and they decided to monitor the development every month.

- They also selected a couple of KPIs to follow up each month. One was the number of customer visits, since they wanted to ensure that they covered all the important customers and branch offices. Another was the increase of business opportunities in numbers and value compared to last year.

- Finally, they put extra focus each month on how the opportunities were progressing by going through these with each sales person. A project list was established through which the sales people reported the status.

The targets and follow-ups increased the focus on sales activities, and most of the employees agreed that the sales culture had developed thanks to the introduction of the new procedures.

As you can see in the examples from the start-up company and the established commercial bank, there are similarities in their approaches. Irrespective of how long you have been on the market, you will be faced with the same types of challenges once sales are being organized.

Meeting structure for a sales organization

A support tool for driving change in a sales organization and to make certain that key tasks are being performed is to plan and carry through the meetings that are required. In figure 13.2 is an example.

Type of meeting	Participants	Agenda
Weekly meeting	Sales Person Sales Manager	The week that passed: Meetings and important events The coming week: Meetings and important events
Monthly business review	Sales Person Sales Manager	Result vs. budget year-to-date Forecast for next month and year-end Opportunity follow-up Coverage of sales territory
Annual review of sales districts	Sales Manager	Reallocation and balancing of workload
Every third year	Corporate Management	Channel strategy (if you are to have a sales force, which parts of the market should it be used on.)

Figure 13.2 Example of a meeting model.

Summary

There is interdependence between the nine dimensions of our model. When introducing the model, you should set the structure first: customer responsibilities, setting targets and basic follow-up procedures. In the next step you establish the on-going management processes with scoreboards, commitment to forecast, follow-up on business opportunities, individual coaching and how to achieve sufficient activity levels. The last step is to introduce quality assurance measures. Scheduled, regular meetings with a thought-through agenda are support tools for making things happen and driving change.

CHAPTER 14

Other implementation tips

In order to increase the productivity in an existing sales organization you are required to change the way you work. It requires a structured approach to lead the organization from the current situation to a future, desired position. In this chapter, we will conclude the book by giving some implementation tips that we have found to work. We will cover:

- The importance of setting a good example.
- Gradual implementation for the people it concerns.
- Gradual implementation of what needs to be done.
- Support by putting pressure.
- Focusing on the "middle".
- Managing expectations.

Setting a good example

Setting a good example in the daily management is key when managing a sales organization. You set an example whenever you interact with the sales person, in all the meetings and coaching sessions, when interacting with colleagues and meeting together with customers.

A manager who doesn't keep the time or honors agreements cannot expect the sales people to do it. A manager that doesn't listen to the sales people cannot expect a sales person to be a good listener. And let's not forget motivation and enthusiasm; enthusiasm is contagious, and when the manager is enthusiastic it leads to positive motivational effects.

Gradual implementation for the people it concerns

New ways of working and new routines could be introduced in one go, but there could also be a gradual implementation where you introduce it to one group at the time. Some things are better implemented when first focusing on a few, and then extending them to a wider audience.

Finding and supporting ambassadors

In most groups, there are some individuals that are more open to and accepting of change. Identifying these individuals and giving them positive attention when they perform in line with the new expectations could be a good way to drive change.

Changing the dress code

The company sold computer systems to the, in clothing terms, more casual university segment as well as more formal ones, such as banks. This was a topic from time to time during the coffee breaks: Should they dress as their customers, or does it matter?

After returning from a position abroad, a previous sales person was promoted to sales manager. In the country where he had worked, the dress code for sales people was formal. Perhaps he had become used to it, or perhaps the dress code had degenerated further among his colleagues during his absence, but it was clearly not in line with the new focus the company had lined out. The sales manager had made up his mind: if you are representing the company, it is better if you are overdressed instead of too relaxed.

He himself wore a suit and tie, and it only took a few days before the first sales person dressed the same way. When he met the "dressed-up" sales person he greeted him with a loud and clear "Good to see you looking like a business man, Robert!"

During the following weeks, more and more formally dressed sales people appeared in the corridors. The manager continued to acknowledge well-dressed colleagues. "Great, now you look like a true business woman, Elisabeth!" At the same time, he was careful not to comment or frown at the more casually dressed sales people.

It was only when less than a third of the sales people remained casually dressed that he started to address the topic with them individually.

Selecting and using high-performing sales people as a good example.

A way that has been used successfully to change direction in a sales force is to define the new direction as particularly challenging and important. Then you handpick a couple of skilled sales people with solid performances, give them training, special attention and possibly extra incentives. The new group becomes an internal high-status group and the new direction becomes attractive also for other parts of the sales organization. After that you roll out the new concept to other parts of the organization.

A version of this is to create test groups or "high performance teams" when you change direction or the way you work. When you have established that these are successful it is then easier to implement in the rest of the organization. Producing relevant KPIs and spreading them in the rest of the organization is an important element of demonstrating the success.

Gradual implementation of what needs to be done

Even if you, as a manager, is convinced that a new practice (for example introducing individual targets) will lead to improved results, it could sometimes be wise to introduce it gradually. Habits, corporate culture, and ways of thinking are generally difficult to change, and too dramatic changes at once could lead to demotivation.

It's important that processes for measuring and reporting are in place before you start holding people accountable for the results. A company who has decided to start measuring activities (for example customer visits) needs to ensure that the reporting system works and that the reports it produces are correct.

Only after that you can start analyzing the numbers and improving the effectiveness. This could then be done by first acknowledging the good results of the top performers, demonstrating the correlation between high activity levels and good results. In the next phase, you focus on the average sales people. In the last phase you focus on those falling behind.

In an organization where you have never measured and tracked results other than on a company level, it would be wise to gradually introduce individual targets, measurements and follow-ups. And in organizations that have gone through major changes or where there is insecurity about the future, new processes and routines could be perceived as particularly threatening. In these cases, the importance of a straight communication, an open discussion and a gradual implementation cannot be stressed enough.

Gradual implementation of targets

The electrical installation company had their stock at several places in the country to be able to provide their local customers with speedy installation services. A natural complement of keeping this stock was to start selling their products to others. Over time, it developed into a full-fledged wholesale business. Because it had grown from being an internal stock there were no sales targets or follow-ups on the external deliveries.

The competitors were highly specialized wholesale companies with a much more developed sales focus when approaching the customers. The consultants that the company had used for auditing their business pointed out that sales targets and follow-up procedures would increase the sales effectiveness.

They discussed how to make this happen. There was a strong team spirit and an atmosphere of cooperation in the company. The question of targets had come up before but had been rejected as they were afraid it would ruin the cooperation between people and units, especially if the targets were individual.

The company decided to make a gradual implementation of targets and follow-up procedures by first introducing a playful sales competition where the different sales groups were competing against each other.

They were tracking and comparing the sales volume for all the groups, irrespective of local conditions and potential. The prizes were symbolic but the prestige of winning became an important incentive, which was expected. The sales competition was very popular, but also led to a discussion that it was a bit unfair given the different market conditions for the groups.

Four months later they introduced a new sales competition where the groups now had different targets based on their local market conditions, and where they competed in how well they achieved their targets percentage-wise. The personnel appreciated the effort that was made in making the competition fairer. After running yet another competition like this, they added an individual element on top of the group targets, where the individual reward was even more symbolic.

It took the company a bit more than two years to fully introduce individual targets and follow-up procedures, but it was done without any demotivation effects.

Support by putting pressure

The sales role contains many challenges. Some of the tasks may be outside of the comfort zone and will simply not be done if the manager is not decisive and does not push the sales person. Examples of this could be calling high status customers, calling dissatisfied customers, or "cold calling" - calls to potential customers the sales person has never met before.

The example below demonstrates that it is not always enough to understand the importance of doing something, to be motivated, and to have the knowledge and competence. To make it happen, it may require a friendly hand on the back to push the sales person out of the comfort zone.

Call the IT manager at the big corporation!

A sales manager narrates:
When I was a sales person myself and had worked for about a year, my manager and I agreed that I should call the IT manager at the big corporation to book a meeting. My manager double-checked with me that I thought it was a good idea, and I did.

At our next weekly meeting, he asked how the call had gone and whether it had resulted in a meeting. I told him I hadn't had the time to do it since I had to work on a big proposal. He understood and said that I should do it by next week. I promised to do this.

At the following weekly meeting, he asked again about the call. I looked down and said there had been a lot of other things on my plate, but that I would call tomorrow. There was an awkward silence in the room.

At the next meeting after this he didn't even ask. Of course, I never called the IT manager at the big corporation.

I remember this situation when I became a sales manager and I decided to be more persistent in supporting my sales people. When the opportunity arose, I acted like this:

- After a week, I asked if there was something the sales person needed to discuss before making the call. The answer from myself when I was a sales person would have been no, and that was typically the answer to me as well.

- "Surely we agreed that you were to make this call" I then asked. When the sales person said yes, my response was: "Then I think you should call right after this meeting."

- I then asked the sales person to come back directly after the call to tell me how it went.

- If the sales person started to give excuses for not calling now, I simply asked: "Do you want us to schedule a time where I could listen and support while you make that call? Or do you want us to go through how you should structure the call?"

This was the push that normally made the sales person call the customer. Superfluous to say, it was usually a happy, relieved and proud sales person that reported back from the call.

Focusing on the "middle"

The American management consultant Peter Drucker has allegedly said: "The task of management is getting extraordinary results with ordinary people". Irrespective if the quote comes from him or not, it is highly relevant. When striving to increase the total performance of a sales organization, the focus should be on improving the productivity of the majority of the sales people, those who are medium performers. Earlier in the chapter we spoke of the importance of having ambassadors and high performing teams leading the way when changing, but to achieve substantial improvement in results for the entire organization, the focus needs to be on the middle.

In larger sales organization, as in the example below, this is clearly illustrated when the performances of the sales people form a normal distribution curve, with a lot of people in the middle, and a diminishing number of people performing high and low respectively. It's a matter of focusing on this "middle" and making them move their performance up to where the high performers are.

In most organizations, however, the focus is not on the middle and management spends a disproportional amount of time on the extreme performers. Either they spend a lot of time on trying to lift the worst performers to an acceptable level, or they are absorbed in the success of the best performers and spend a lot of time with these.

If they instead focus on the middle, they are in a significantly better position to improve the results. A moderate performance increase from the majority of the sales force in the middle will give a better effect on results, compared to lifting a couple of high performers (who are already performing very well) or lifting a few low performers to acceptable levels (who are unlikely to have the ability to improve).

Focusing on the middle means that you avoid the pitfall of over focusing on high and low performers, and instead free up time to ensure that you really work with and develop the middle. This means prioritizing this group when coaching and doing follow-ups and joint customer calls. This also means that the sales training programs the company runs should have a focus on the middle, enabling the improvement of the vast majority of the sales people.

Moving the middle

The company, which sold heavy equipment, had decided to launch an improvement program for their sales force. The focus of the program initiated a lively discussion in the management meeting. Someone thought they should simply cut loose and terminate all the low performers, while someone else believed that success lay in making the stars perform even better.

This time the CFO and the sales director could agree on what they believed was the right way – to focus on the performance of the majority of the sales people, those in the middle.

For the sales director, it was based on previous experience and a firm belief in the importance for management getting the majority on board.

For the CFO, focusing on and improving the middle simply made sense from a mathematical standpoint.

During the management meeting it was agreed that the CFO and the sales director were to simulate and analyze the outcome of the proposed changes and to present these at the next meeting.

The analysis gave the following results:

The company had 71 sales people selling for an average of 25 MEUR, with the performances distributed according to figure 14.1.

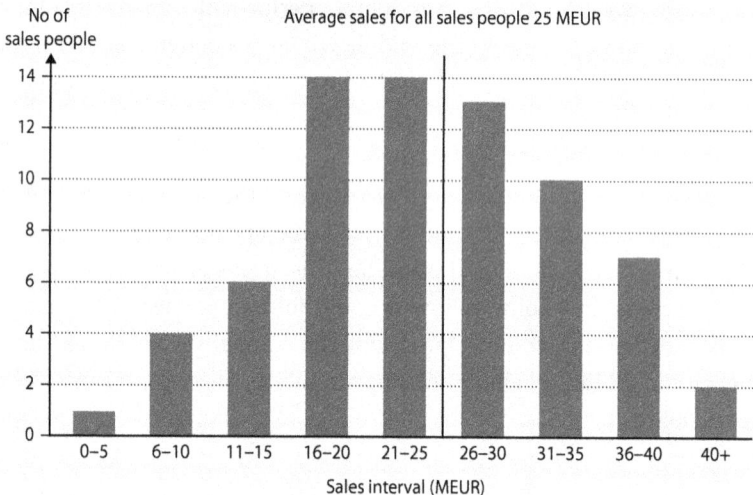

Figure 14.1 Performances distributed according to sales intervals

In the planned improvement program, with the ambition set to grow 15%, the strategy was to focus on the middle (figure 14.2). They assumed the high performing sales people were to maintain their performance and that it would be unlikely for the low performers to improve, even if they were in focus.

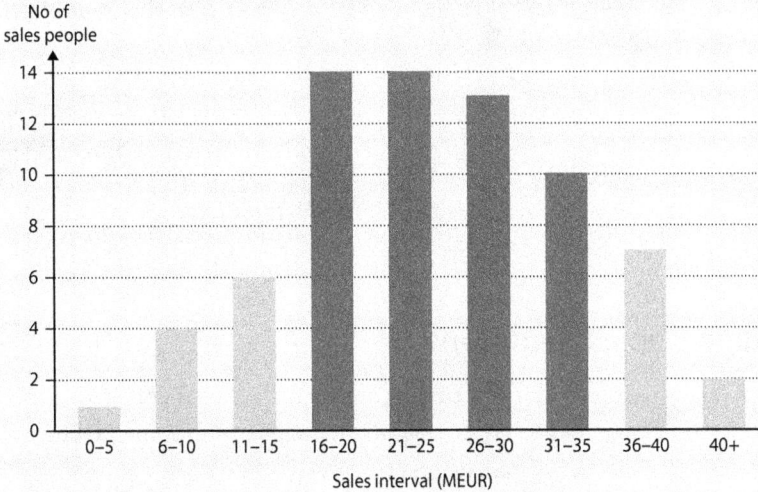

Figure 14.2 Focusing on the sales people in the middle

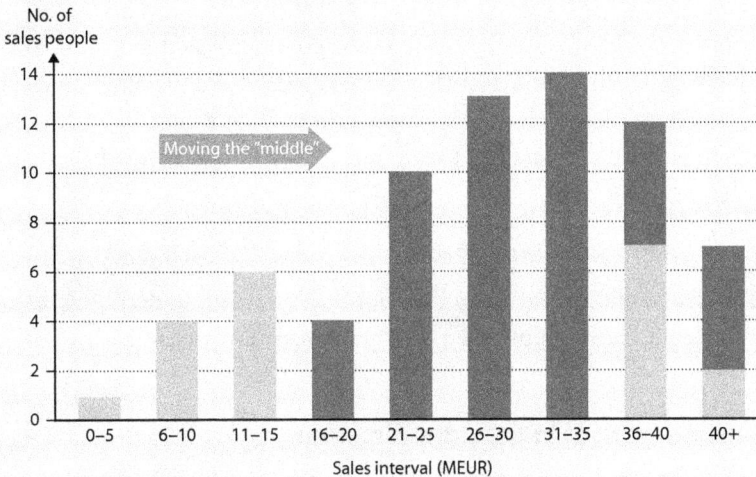

Figure 14.3 Moving the sales people in the middle

If the program succeeded the middle would shift, and their performances would be closer to, and even overlap, those of the high performers (figure 14.3).

This meant that the company would increase by 266 MEUR or 15 %, which would be achieved by the sales people in the "middle" improving their average sales by 22 %.

Had the high performers alone driven the same improvement, they would have been forced to increase their performance by 62 %. And if the company had relied on the low performers alone, they would've been forced to step up their performance by 214 %.

The decision at the next meeting to focus on the middle was an easy one.

Managing expectations

Clear expectations and requirements are important elements in our model and its nine dimensions. We conclude this chapter with some practical tips regarding this aspect of management.

Be clear on all expectations and requirements

Expectations and requirements should be communicated in a straight and simple manner to ensure that they are received and understood correctly. When communicating verbally, confirm important things in writing: formally in target documents and such, informally through e-mail.

Follow up on big things and small

We have covered this earlier in the book, but it's worth underlining the importance of following up – even the small everyday things.

Turning demands in the right direction

It is not unusual for managers of sales organizations to end up in situations where the demands, expectations and sometimes dissatisfaction of the sales people dominate: "We have to have lower prices", "Our products are too old", and "The support doesn't work, so I can't sell anything more to the customer". The manager should of course try to resolve true problems, but it's vital for driving change that it is the manager's demands and expectations that dominate the picture.

That the atmosphere sometimes becomes negative can happen in a demanding environment such as a sales organization. That there is muttering and complaining instead of constructive work could be a sign of serious problems that need to be addressed.

But it could also be a sign of a temporary slump from individuals or groups. If you can determine it being a temporary slump, and not a serious or real problem, it is effective to turn the demands in the other direction. The demands are then turned away from the management and to the sales people instead. The way to do this is to increase the demands and expectations so the sales people will refocus their attention, from being dissatisfied to being busy delivering on the new expected levels. Successful managers always make sure that the expectations are turned in the right direction.

Summary

To set a good example is a key aspect in managing sales people. To make coaching and follow-ups work it is vital that the manager acts the way he or she wishes the sales people to act, for example by being a good listener, by being on time, and not least, by being enthusiastic about the job.

Changes are best implemented gradually by firstly focusing on a few people and then increasing the number of people involved. Gradual implementation also works well, introducing new working practices and methods step-by-step.

Some tasks may be so far out of the comfort zone that they will not be done unless the manager pushes the sales person until they are completed.

The focus, when increasing the sales effectiveness, should be on the vast majority of the sales people that are in the middle, by enabling them to improve their productivity and working methods.

Clarity in formulating expectations and demands, and to follow-up on these, are success factors.

NOTES

1. Matthew Dixon & Brent Adamson (2001), *"The Challenger Sale"*

2. Andris A. Zoltners, Prabhakant Sinha & Greggor A. Zoltners (2001) *"The Complete Guide to Accelerating Sales Force Performance"*

3. Andris A. Zoltners, Prabhakant Sinha & Greggor A. Zoltners (2001) *"The Complete Guide to Accelerating Sales Force Performance"*. p. 30

4. W.R. Smith, *"Product Differentiation and Market Segmentation as Alternative Marketing Strategies"*, Journal of Marketing, 21 July (1956) p. 3-8

5. Y. Wind & R. Cardozo, *"Industrial Market Segmentation"*, Industrial Marketing Management, 3 (1974) p. 153-166

6. Magnus Söderlund, *"Den lojala kunden"*, Liber (2001) p. 187-210

7. Sahlgren & Skog, *"Belöningssystem i svenska säljkårer"*, 2008

8. Carl-Johan Petri & Nils-Göran Olve, *"Balanserad styrning: Utveckling och tillämpning i svensk praktik"*, (2014), p. 7-9.

9. Jeffrey N. Rouder, Richard D. Morey, Nelson Cowan (2008), *"An assessment of fixed-capacity models of visual working memory"*. Graem S. Halford, Rosemary Baker, Julie E. McCredden, John D. Bain (2005) *"How much can your mind keep track of?"*

10. Yemm, Graham (2013). *"Essential Guide to Leading Your Team : How to Set Goals, Measure Performance and Reward Talent."* Pearson Education. p. 37–39.

11. Dan Ariely, Emir Kamenica, Drazen Prelec (2008) *"Man's search for meaning: The case of Legos"*

12. Sahlgren & Skog, *"Belöningssystem i svenska säljkårer"*, 2008

13. Daniel H. Pink *"Drive: The Surprising Truth About What Motivates Us"*, 5 april (2011)

14. Sahlgren & Skog, *"Belöningssystem i svenska säljkårer"*, 2008

15. Hackman, J.R. & Oldham, G.R. (1980) *"Work redesign"* Reading, Mass.:Addison-Wesley.

16. Robinson, Farris & Wind (1967 s.14) and Kotler, Armstrong & Perment (2013 2. 180-183).

17. Skinner, B.F. (1938), *"The Behavior of Organisms"*, New York: Appleton-Century-Crofts.

18. Corcoran, Kevin J., Laura K. Petersen, Daniel B. Baitch, and Mark Barrett (1995), *"High-Performance Sales Organizations: Achieving Competitive Advantage in the Global Marketplace"*, Chicago: Irwin Professional Publications.

19. Jaworsky B.J., Kohli A.K. (1991), *"Supervisory Feedback: Alternative types and Their Impact on Salespeople's Performance and Satisfaction"*, Journal of Marketing Research.

20. Kaplan, Robert S. and Bruns, W. *"Accounting and Management: A Field Study Perspective"* (Harvard Business School Press, 1987)

21. Magnus Söderlund, *"Den lojala kunden"*, Liber (2003) p. 189-198

INDEX